What Others Are Saying
about John Craig and This Book

"John was the best leader I encountered at the Boeing Company. Folks who worked for him all loved and appreciated his endearing style. He is both a can-do, tactical manager and a strategic visionary who easily operates in both of those dissimilar worlds. He was my customer at one point and my manager at another. During my darkest hour at Boeing, John saved my career. I shall always be grateful for his 'Braveheart' maneuver that kept me at Boeing, ultimately creating a crucial strategy and building an indispensable global, non-profit organization to secure the aviation industry. The Aviation Information Sharing and Analysis Center (A-ISAC) has been the reason the aviation industry has not had a cyber 9-11. Enjoy John's storytelling and no-nonsense, clever manner in communicating his wisdom."

Faye Francy,
Executive Director, Automotive Information Sharing
and Analysis Center, Former Boeing Director

"John Craig is the recognized expert for the United States. I always appreciated his ability to work effectively with different government entities and help frame the industries' cyber framework for aviation. He was respected and able to bring different government agencies together to address the cyber threat to commercial aviation."

Fred Schwien,
Director Government Affairs, Boeing

"John has the unique ability to examine complex cabin avionics problems, and through teamwork, planning, and implementation, he has expeditiously arrived at the best solution while meeting Boeing requirements. He possesses a vast knowledge of airplane cabin avionics systems and was always a creative thinker and sought-after problem solver."

Lori Salazar,
Software Support, TimeTap and Former Vice President of Product
Management, Thales Avionics

"I first met John when I worked at the Department of Homeland Security and quickly became impressed with his ability to communicate and work across many different stakeholders involved in aviation and cybersecurity. He was recognized as a thought leader in the space and was instrumental in building an early framework for a joint public-private sector approach for securing the aviation industry from cyber threats."

Monica Maher,
Senior Vice President Goldman Sachs, Former Director of Operations,
Department of Homeland Security

"As surprising as it may sound, friendships exist even between competitors in business. My and John Craig's mutual trust has been the basis of our long relationship and has never wavered. We have both always worked for the good cause—that of better air transport safety—both for our customers and for passengers. I keep the image of John as an excellent traveling companion, one on whom it is easy to rest, not only thanks to his stature but above all for his professionalism and his increased knowledge of the systems on board our beautiful flying machines and his experience as a benchmark engineer. Cyber threats have no borders; we both understood it, and we have been united to challenge them together."

Pascal Andrei,
Chief Security Officer, Airbus

"John frequently demonstrated his unique ability to tell a story while weaving it into a higher-level message, often with a morality tale. He was able to couple his gift of storytelling with a wealth of experiences from his rural upbringing to frame a 'big picture' that resonated with his intended audience. At Boeing, he had a variety of assignments that allowed him to experience many of the different aspects of designing and building airplanes along with navigating other aspects of the aviation ecosystem. Over the years, he had many unique experiences and contributions that only those within the aviation community were aware of or could appreciate. In his book, John relates some of these experiences with a twist of humor, and as he is prone to do, with an underlying message. John was a capable and respected leader at Boeing and enjoyed support from his peers and coworkers. I think you will greatly enjoy the lessons he has learned from his stories of growing up in Montana to his time spent at Boeing."

Todd Zarfos,
Retired Boeing Engineering Vice President,
Washington Design Center

"John Craig's insider stories about working at Boeing will please any fan of aviation. From designing safety features to owning his mistakes and marveling at the wonder of man able to fly, John propels the reader forward, making it hard to put the book down. Plus *Life Lessons Learned the Hard Way* makes the lessons not only easy but fun to learn."

Tyler R. Tichelaar, PhD
Award-Winning Author of *When Teddy Came to Town*

"*Life Lessons Learned the Hard Way* is filled with nuggets of truth hidden within John Craig's enjoyable stories about his many experiences from growing up in Montana to working with Boeing. You'll find out how he learned why not to lie to the police, how to be a good manager, and how to stand up to bullies, whether you are a kid or an adult. This book will have you flying high with its humor and honesty."

Nicole Gabriel
Author of *Finding Your Inner Truth* and *Stepping Into Your Becoming*

"John Craig's tales from his impressive career at Boeing alone make this book worth reading, but on top of that, there are stories of growing up in the 1970s, fraternity antics, cantankerous people he's had to deal with throughout his life, and some homespun truths you won't want to miss. *Life Lessons Learned the Hard Way* will be a great tool to help you on your own path through life."

Patrick Snow,
Publishing Coach and International Bestselling Author of *Creating Your Own Destiny* and *The Affluent Entrepreneur*

LIFE LESSONS
LEARNED THE HARD WAY

**SHORT STORIES ON
LEADERSHIP FROM
A MONTANAN AND
AVIATION EXECUTIVE**

JOHN CRAIG

AVIVA
PUBLISHING
New York

LIFE
LESSONS
LEARNED THE HARD WAY

LIFE LESSONS LEARNED THE HARD WAY
Short Stories on Leadership from a Montanan and Aviation Executive

Copyright © 2022 by John Craig. All rights reserved.

Published by:
Aviva Publishing
Lake Placid, NY 12946
(518) 523-1320
www.AvivaPubs.com

John Craig
john@johncraigconsulting.com
www.JohnCraigConsulting.com
www.JohnCraigLessons.com
www.LifeLessonsLearnedTheHardWay.com

ISBN: 978-1-63618-153-0
Library of Congress: 2021923967

Editors: Tyler Tichelaar and Larry Alexander, Superior Book Productions
Cover Designer: Nicole Gabriel, Angel Dog Productions
Interior Book Layout: Nicole Gabriel, Angel Dog Productions
Author Photo: Barb White

Every attempt has been made to properly source all quotes.
Some names of individuals have been changed to protect their privacy.
Printed in the United States of America
First Edition

4 6 8 10 12 14

DEDICATION

This book is dedicated to my mother, Karol Craig (1940–1993). Her perseverance, frustration, and many years of raising three boys molded my childhood and, ultimately, my success.

Part of my mother's frustration was her daily experiences as we grew up, including often having to visit the school or talk to the occasional police officer who came to our door. Some of these events are captured in this book while others are reserved for a future time. At one Christmas Eve dinner when we were older, Mother became very upset, threw down her fork, and cursed us: "I hope when you grow up, you all have nothing but girls, and they put you through the same hell you boys put me through." This became known in the family as the "Curse of Karol." Sure enough, the first five grandchildren were girls with only number six, the last, being a boy. We theorized that his birth meant our mother above had finally forgiven us.

This book also goes out to all my distant relatives who captured their stories about coming to America and to their children for editing and publishing their experiences. Reading through them became my real motivation for writing this book, something I would dabble with on long business flights and to record stories about my daughters and the reality of the Curse of Karol.

Last, I need to acknowledge my wife Bonnie's contribution to this book and living the experiences with me. She has listened to many of these stories, some multiple times, and lived several with me in the years we've been together. Without her patience and understanding, this would have been a much more difficult task to complete.

ACKNOWLEDGMENTS

Many people contributed to this book—too many to mention—but I will acknowledge a few who played pivotal roles. First, I'd like to thank Diana Ruiz for introducing me to Patrick Snow. Patrick guided me through the process to successfully publish the book you now hold. Second, I'd like to thank the many employees and managers at Boeing whom I had the privilege of working with over the many years. Aviation is unique and one of the few industries in which you will see people work their entire careers. Last, I'd like to thank my family, especially Bonnie, my wife, for supporting me these many years and helping get this book over the finish line.

I would also like to thank Tyler Tichelaar and Larry Alexander for their amazing editing skills. Without their talent, this book would just be an incomplete Word document on my laptop. In addition, I would like to thank Nicole Gabriel for her amazing work on the cover and interior art. She was able to transform my vision into something that captured both my upbringing in Montana and my love of aviation from a young age.

CONTENTS

INTRODUCTION

The world today is about as divisive as it has ever been. The advent of social media and "big tech" have changed how we communicate, and some people even think those industries are now controlling what we think. With this new way to communicate, it seems we are communicating less. Writing has been replaced with small snippets of video and short text messages. Polls show that those who spend more time with family and friends on weekends are happier and have less stress than those who report being alone all day. Common sense, right, but we also seemed to have lost our common sense. We all have had bosses we didn't like, and many today live in fear of losing their jobs, even those whose jobs aren't really at risk. We think the kids don't listen, people don't respect me…the list goes on.

How do you break free from all this stress? What if you could go back in time to give yourself advice, knowing what you do today? What would you tell yourself? What changes would you make? At work, do you wish you had more control over your career?

I've had these thoughts myself. I've thought about what I would do differently if I could go back in time, knowing what I know today. I have had money problems, had bosses I didn't really like, and learned the hard way that raising a family is much more difficult than it appears.

Working at a large aerospace company, I rose up through the ranks, and in the final years of my career, I had a respectable position in the company.

I would often be asked how I reached that position. After I talked with several people, it dawned on me that I probably had some "aha" moments I could share with others, along with career and general life advice.

In this book, I will share my life lessons and many of the things I learned along the way. I will share stories from my past and work life that I hope you can relate to and in some manner translate to your personal experience, opening your horizons to things that may help you. I grew up in a unique time and a special place that was forgiving of mistakes and helped reenforce positive messages. We seem to have lost that general sense of kindness and the ability to help the next generation learn and go through some of the same life experiences that made up who we are.

I grew up in the open spaces of Montana. I drove hundreds of miles as a teenager to go skiing or travel to other parts of the state. I attended college in Bozeman, Montana, and received a degree in electrical engineering from Montana State University. After being hired by the Boeing Company right after college, I worked on pretty much all the commercial airplanes flying today. In my thirty-five years at Boeing, I rose from being one of thousands of engineers to being an executive responsible for the airplane networks and cyber security group tasked with securing airplane systems.

During this time, I traveled the world, met with government leaders, and spoke at many industry forums. Along the way, I learned how to interact with people, both employees and those from distant cultures. In my time, I had to deal with very difficult employees and situations that required a softer touch. Managing people is one of the more difficult things I've done, and over many years, I learned things I will share here. I don't pretend to have all the answers—I am on a life journey like everyone else.

I hope you enjoy reading my stories and find some humor in them. I've recorded events as I remember them, and I tried not to embellish them the way I do when talking to my friends. As you read, I hope you see the book's overarching messages that carry from chapter to chapter. This was not by design, but over the years, these messages were reenforced, and once I became aware of them, I became a better father, husband, and manager. The messages here are not specifically work-related, but I use work experiences to highlight them. My hope is these messages will smooth your life's path, and you will become a better person or help another become a better person. If that happens, I will have achieved my goal in writing this book.

I've included some exercises at the end of each chapter to help you reflect. I hope they add value and help you understand the messages better.

Also, as Sergeant Joe Friday from the TV show *Dragnet* said, "The names have been changed to protect the innocent." The same is true here. While all the characters in this book are real, I have modified their descriptions to protect their identities.

Alwarq

"Those who cannot remember the past are condemned to repeat it!"

— George Santayana

CHAPTER 1

NOT EVERYBODY LIKES ME

"It is better to be hated for what you are
than to be loved for what you are not."

— André Gide, author of *Autumn Leaves*

REALIZATION

It can be hard when you realize your worldview is wrong, and even harder to realize your view of your role in the world is incorrect. If we come into this life being loved and have a positive upbringing, it is easy for us to assume everyone must feel loved. (There are other books that can help with the opposite, and I am not going to be of help here.) My life has generally been positive and one I'm thankful for. We all have challenges, but from looking at the people who influenced my life and how they interacted with me, I learned an important lesson on how we interact with the people we are influencing. I often tell my daughters that whom you associate with will greatly impact your success.

I grew up in a magical time in probably the best place in the world—Montana. It was the 1970s and 1980s, and people were generally happy. There was an order to life, and we all understood what it was. If you were polite, people were polite back. Even the police got respect, and if you gave them respect, they would often look at the bigger picture and ignore minor indiscretions. This was a time when you could walk to school for fifteen to thirty minutes, starting in elementary school, with no fear. I walked to school by myself my first day of first grade. (At least I thought I was by myself—I'm sure my mother was following discretely.) I knew where to go and felt grown up doing it by myself. Even with the oil embargo of the 1970s, all seemed to be at peace in the universe. (I do recall looking back once while walking to school during the oil embargo. I watched cars drive by and thought, *Will I ever get to drive?* I thought cars would not exist when I got older.)

One day in second grade, I got into a fight with a friend like school children do, but this fight was different. After the fact, I would realize he probably did not have a positive upbringing. I could not understand where he was coming from when he started throwing rocks at me, something I had not experienced prior. I was upset and ran home, wondering what had happened. Upon my reaching home, my mother comforted me, but she told me not everyone would like me and that was part of life. I could not believe her—how could this be true? The next day in school when I approached "my friend," he seemed to be okay, but after a few hours, he started picking on me again. This was different—I was a well-liked kid who had lots of friends. I noticed soon after that he didn't. While walking home, I went by his house and his older brother started yelling at me. I did not know his brother, but it dawned on me that my mother was right—a hard reality that started to change my perspective of the world. How could it be that everyone couldn't get along and like each other? I had a difficult time with this concept for quite a while. I distanced myself from "my friend" and started paying attention to how others were treating me. I focused on working on those relationships.

I think we all come to this realization at some point: Everyone is unique and has a different perspective on life. At Boeing, as with other companies, we are put through diversity training, where the focus is on the color of your skin or gender. I've learned over time that diversity is really not about color or gender; it is about who we are and how we interact with each other. One trainer summarized it perfectly. She said 90 percent of a person's uniqueness cannot be seen. To highlight this point, she described how different people who may look alike can be very different, and she gave several examples. One was how someone from Russia may never admit a mistake or ask for help. In their culture, it could mean a death sentence or a trip to Siberia.

TREATING ALL WITH RESPECT AND DIGNITY

After reflecting in second grade on my newfound knowledge, I wasn't quite sure how to interact with "my friend" if we did get together somehow in school. I had already broken off my after-school contact with him, and I wanted to be prepared for any issues in school. I was pretty upset with him and really didn't want to see him at all. I even went so far as to think about actually engaging him in a fight. A few months later, he approached me at recess and caught me by surprise. I was still pretty upset with him, but he asked why we didn't do anything after school anymore. It was as if he didn't recall what he had done or the words we had exchanged. At this point, I had a decision to make—should I be hostile to him or have a civil discussion with him? I listened to him, but before I could make a decision, recess was over and he left. This interaction really did not change my feelings about him, but I did realize the door was open in the future if things changed.

While I was growing up, my father was often away working. He was a highway contractor and always on the job site, which was often one hundred to two hundred miles away. Since I was the oldest child, his absence probably shaped how I interact with people. As I got older, I found I had an ability to communicate with my peers and their parents effectively. By comparison, my younger brother often got in trouble because he did not understand how to interact with my mother as an adult. Funny thing is he is now a lawyer and probably the best in the family at interacting with people.

As I got older and started to drive, I was cut loose on the open highways. During the oil embargo, the nation put in place a 55-mph speed limit. Montana did as well, but it had a twist. First, a violation of the speed limit was not a moving violation; it was "an unnecessary waste of a natural resource." Second, the fine was five dollars. I have a file folder of speeding tickets for five dollars, the highest being for going 92 mph in a 55-mph zone. (This habit came back to sting me when I moved to Washington State; they had a different perspective, so I came close to getting a habitual offender violation with four tickets within about a year.) That said, I spent a lot of time in highway patrol cars. Talking to the officers was pretty pleasant and more of a social experience than anything else.

One summer, my father became weary of me hanging out around the pool and got me a construction job in Rock Springs, Wyoming. Rock Springs was about 380 miles from our home, and it took me six hours to drive there each way. Rock Springs was a desolate place, but interesting people lived there. When I first arrived, it was late at night, and I got a room at the Thunderbird Motor Inn. This was the kind of motel where you park in front of your door.

The guy in the room next to me worked construction as well and, returning from work, I'd find him on a lawn chair on the sidewalk between his room and his truck. I thought that was a good idea and got myself a lawn chair.

One day, I got back to the motel early, before he was out on his chair. About thirty minutes later, a large woman of the night opened his door and walked by, asking how I was doing. He came out after with a smile on his face. I was a little surprised since up to then, I had lived a somewhat sheltered life.

About a week later, one of the women on the crew told me she'd been loading her boyfriend's bullets with rubber tips. I asked her why. I knew a bit about firearms and loading, but I had never heard of loading rubber-tipped bullets before. She said her boyfriend was going to the local bar the next weekend, and if he shot anyone, he wouldn't kill them.

Rock Springs was a unique place, and I really didn't want to spend much time there.

When driving home, I would drive as fast as I could. I was pulled over a few times in Wyoming, and I learned a couple of important lessons. Number one, be polite.

One day, driving through a small town, my radar detector went off, and I immediately hit the brakes. The local police officer pulled out behind me and followed me out of the town about ten miles beyond the city limits. When he pulled me over, I watched him get out of his car.

At the time, I was twenty and had already received some traffic tickets. The officer immediately asked me how fast I was going. I responded in a respectful, but humorous way, that I had been doing the speed limit. I thought, *What's the difference? He's going to give me a ticket anyway, and it won't hurt to lighten the mood.*

I could tell he had a sense of humor, and we bantered back and forth about the speed limit and why I had slowed down so sharply. Then he asked me to join him in his car. The story I tell my friends is much longer, but in this shortened version, after about an hour sitting in his car discussing the finer points of Wyoming, where I was going to school, and how his radio worked, he said, "You don't look like the kind of guy a speeding ticket would do much good. Where would you be right now if you hadn't been speeding through my town?"

"I'd be home," I said.

"So, it doesn't really pay to speed through my town, now does it?" he said and let me go.

At that time, the ticket would have probably cost me between $50 and $100—a lot to a college student in the 1980s. Wow, by being respectful and interacting the right way, I had actually talked my way out of a ticket. The sixty minutes in his car was a long time (especially for the passenger in my car wondering what was going on), but I've gotten more than my money's worth out of this story over time.

This experience also taught me to religiously drive slowly through small towns.

The second lesson here is always to carry cash when driving. This is another story I could write an entire chapter on, but essentially, I was pulled over for speeding in Wyoming on the open highway. The patrol officer did not have a sense of humor, and I think he was at the end of his shift. Since I didn't have cash to pay the fine, I would have to spend the weekend in Lander, Wyoming, until the judge could see me on Monday. I did talk the officer into driving into a small town to see if I could get the cash. At the time, ATMs were just being deployed but hadn't yet made it to Wyoming. After checking a few gas stations, I went into a bar and asked if they would cash a check—they said no.

Then I asked for a shot of tequila in preparation for going to jail. The bartender and patrons were aware I had pulled in with the Wyoming Highway Patrol and decided to cash my check, saving me from incarceration. I paid the patrolman, and upon leaving, thanked him and said they should paint their police cars so you could see them more easily (forgetting he had no sense of humor).

He just said, "If you are going to drive like that in my great state, I suggest you carry more cash," and left.

During my high school and college years, I began to understand the importance and advantages of getting along with everyone—those I liked, and those I knew didn't like me. At Billings West High School, we had "jocks" and "freaks." I was probably more aligned with the jocks, but I spent a lot of time with the freaks.

High school is a time when a young man's testosterone is peaking and you are assigned your "pecking order." Your place corresponds with the company you keep, how you handle yourself, and your physical presence. I was never really into fighting and had seen the negative results of a fight, even for the winner, a few times. The saying goes, "Nobody ever wins a fight," and there is truth to that.

When I was in high school, the drinking age was nineteen, but it wasn't really enforced, so in my later years of high school, I would indulge in the spirits regularly. By the time I got to college, when it was legal, drinking wasn't really a novelty anymore. During those impressionable years from high school through college, I fine-tuned my ability to reason with all sorts of people, both sober and intoxicated—them and me. I could get between friends and talk them down from fighting; when strangers challenged me, I could divert their attention to something else. I also helped my friends meet girls, which earned me some respect and loyalty.

I wasn't on the top of the pecking order, but I was close to it. I was also able to work with the different groups at school, even those I had no intention of interacting with on a deeper level. They knew this and were okay with it.

This ability to fit in with diverse groups and mediate conflict continued into college, and I began to see and understand an even larger picture. At Montana State, I joined the Sigma Alpha Epsilon Fraternity. It was probably the best time of my life. I'll document my fraternal experiences in a later book. For now, I'll say that many of my classmates' fathers had been members of the same fraternity at the same time. Many had become influential people. They were interested in not only helping their children, but also their children's classmates succeed. In the fraternity, I developed lifelong friendships with many who have gone on to become very successful. Outside of the military, this was the closest you could get to a "Band of Brothers." Thirty-five years later, many of my fraternity brothers are still very close friends. Ensuring positive relationships with these individuals from the start has helped me personally and financially a few times. And some of these fraternity friends would go on to help my friends just because the person in need knew me. That is a powerful bond.

After college, in the working world, respect is even more important. You are in an environment where your superiors can dramatically affect your career, your compensation, and promotions. The interesting thing about the work environment is the management chain. Before you join the workforce, your position with peers is based largely on your age. At work, a key to getting along and doing well is understanding your employee may become your boss.

I have seen some rise to significant positions and, in the process, leave a lot of damage in their wake. One boss in my area, a new executive, experienced the negative result of not cultivating positive relationships with everyone. One of his employees became his boss, and others who were promoted above him remembered him. He was essentially pushed out. This happened during a culture change at Boeing, and I saw many theory X managers, those who didn't think it necessary to promote positive relationships with coworkers or "underlings," depart the company.

It's like the saying, "From the ranks you have risen, and to the ranks you shall return." At the end of the day, we will all be held accountable for how we treat others, either while working or after. I understood this early on.

SUMMARY

The lessons here are simple:

Everyone has a perspective and situation they are dealing with.

My grade school friend probably wasn't really that bad, and I think he wanted to make amends. The first police officer probably had some time on his hands, and I think he enjoyed the interaction. With the second officer, it was apparent he really didn't want to deal with me, but he couldn't ignore the infraction. He had better things to do, and spending time with me was not on his list.

Having an open mind and looking for the best in people is imperative to a happy, successful life.

Try to understand people's situations and look for ways to help them in how you interact. If they are in a hurry, help them move along. If they attack you, don't aggravate the situation. If they express interest in you, take time to interact with them.

Life is about interacting with different people and their perspectives.

It's important to be able to discuss ideas and different views in a collaborative way. We must understand that no solution will please everyone, so we must come to an agreement that helps all accept the change and move forward.

By not making a decision, you are effectively making one.

One of the most powerful lessons I've learned is the concept of making a decision. By not making a decision, you have actually made one. Part of making a decision is also accepting that your decision may be wrong and being able to change as new information becomes available.

EXERCISES

1. When did you realize or have you realized you can't please everyone?

   _____

   _____

   _____

   _____

2. How do you interact with someone who is diametrically opposed to your perspective?

   _____

   _____

   _____

   _____

3. Describe a situation that went well based on your positive outlook on the interaction.

   _____

   _____

   _____

   _____

CHAPTER 2

THE CRAZY LADY
ON THE HILL

"When you argue with an idiot, you have to ask
yourself who is the real idiot."

— Clifford Craig (my grandfather)

FORMING THE ASSOCIATION

My brothers and I purchased twenty acres outside of Seattle, Washington, in the Cascades. We did this as an investment, but also a getaway. Eight lots were sold, and soon after we purchased, the developer hosted a new owners' meeting with the outcome being us creating a homeowners association (HOA). The purpose of the homeowners association was enumerated in the CC&Rs (Covenants, Conditions & Restrictions) and included many rules that most other HOAs were held to. Being a remote place with twenty-acre parcels, the only real requirement and desire the members had was that the road be maintained, which initially, meant plowing during the winter. In forming the association, I volunteered to be on the board and was elected as president.

During the association's first meeting, everyone was pretty upbeat, looking forward to building structures and enjoying the great outdoors. One couple, though, started asking interesting questions upfront that, in retrospect, foreshadowed the struggles we would have with them. The comment that struck me the most came after I described what I was going to do. Mr. Anderson said, "We'll have to see about that," implying he was in charge, even though he was not elected to the board.

When we started, nobody really had experience with running an association, and we didn't have much legal input on how to run it. We essentially formed a non-profit, limited liability company (LLC), opened a checking account, and collected money to pay for snowplowing. We did engage a lawyer to write up the articles of incorporation and by-laws, but that was essentially it.

Later, I learned we were not running the HOA even close to the letter of the law, but life was okay with plowing the road. The owners on the top, the Andersons, owned a consulting firm, had a formal relationship with the local university, and a relationship with a timber company that had property bordering ours. Mr. Anderson talked in the meetings as if he understood all the legal implications. And when he started to build, he sued most of his sub-contractors at the end for poor quality or something similar. If you have lived in a small town, you know this kind of activity is noticed, and soon he had a reputation for suing people.

THE WELL

Part of developing raw property is bringing in services, including power, water, a septic system, and cable/internet/telephone. The original property owner who had developed the twenty-acre parcels had put in a road system, power, and telephones at each of the primary lot sites originally envisioned. This meant to effectively build you needed water and a septic system. Septic systems had been put in for many other developments and lots, so a septic system was not really a risk. The risk was water.

Those who put in wells are told right upfront that the driller does not provide any guarantee of finding water. When it came time to drill my well, my driller, "Waterman" recommended I hire a water witch for $150. Being an engineer by trade, I didn't really believe the witch was anything more than a gimmick, but he convinced me and commented that everywhere he told people to drill, they found water. Those who didn't use the witch usually got a dry hole. Since we were looking at ten to fifteen thousand for the well, I figured I'd invest $150—if anything, it would be entertaining.

The water witch arrived on the hill with a fresh branch from a tree he had grown in his yard. (He told me the kind of tree that worked best, but I forget.) He took the branch, bent the "y" in it, and held it, separating the "y" in each fist with the straight end of the branch straight ahead. He walked and the branch mysteriously bent down, calling out "here." I marked the spot with blue spray paint. I didn't believe he could find water and watched him closely to see if he was moving his hands or manipulating the stick in any way, but I couldn't see anything.

The stick bent down again—more blue spray paint. After about fifteen minutes, and not paying attention to the dots' locations, we had marked about twenty dots on the ground. Stepping back, we saw they were all in a line. Waterman announced this was where we should drill—we hit an underground stream. We drilled and got water with fairly good flow.

Ironically, the neighbor next to me hired an engineering firm to locate her well. They marked it on the same line and she got water.

Why do I tell this story? The Andersons were the first to purchase, with most others following in the next few months. Part of their purchase and sale agreement was putting in a well that produced a specified amount, which it did. Everyone else took a chance without requiring a well be put in. A well at the time cost around $15,000 and could go down 200 to 400 feet. Ours went down 440 feet with our standing water level around 220 feet. When the second neighbor put their well down next to the Andersons, they got forty gallons a minute—a very good well and much more than the Andersons. When the third property owner had the well driller working on their property, Mr. Anderson went to the drillers as they were drilling on the third owner's property and informed them they could not drill there. They were taking from his water.

Threatening legal letters were exchanged, and Anderson backed down when the property owner drafted a letter from his legal team. He was the CFO at a national telecom and probably had access to more prominent lawyers. At that stage, it became obvious that the Andersons were world-class bullies who threatened people with legal action as a matter of course.

SNOWMOBILES AND SNOWPLOWING

The association's single task was to plow the roads in winter. With the roads recently graded, they did not really need much attention early on. The roads were pretty steep in some areas and narrow in other places. Part of living up there was owning a 4x4 to access the properties in the winter. Prior to houses being built on top of the hill, the locals would snowmobile up the roads to access hundreds of acres of snowmobile trails and fields. All those who were building up there had plans to purchase snowmobiles and ride them—using the primary roads to access the groomed trails. With a large development below our property, there were also several hundred homes with similar plans, and our property had historically been used by these folks to access the snowmobile trails.

As we entered our first year, the Andersons took issue with the snowmobiles on the roads. In meetings, they demanded we keep them off the roads, and in one meeting, they brought their lawyer to convey the message. They commented that it was in their purchase and sale agreement; therefore, it was not allowed. Those who have purchased real estate know the purchase and sale agreement is the legal document between the seller and buyer and does not typically have any restrictions on use of the property. Use is controlled by homeowners associations or covenants that run with the land. When I brought this up to the Andersons and their lawyer, the lawyer confirmed my observation. I asked them to no longer bring up the subject. Snowmobiles were allowed with a few restrictions.

In a small town, those who like you will help you and do things they probably shouldn't. After this exchange, I inquired with the real estate agent to see if the Andersons had any "snowmobile" language in their purchase and sale agreement. They had none. The Andersons were now documented liars.

The snowmobile issue continued with Mr. Anderson blocking the road at the bottom with his car to prevent snowmobiles from coming up. I watched it once—it was comical since they just drove around his car. On one occasion, Anderson confronted a snowmobiler and apparently got into a fight with him, getting his jaw broken. I didn't really know Anderson's age, but I would guess he was close to sixty. I don't know anyone else that age who still starts fights.

The Andersons decided to put a gate up on the road on their property line to block snowmobiles. It didn't affect me, but it impaired access to three other lots with cabins. The gate became an issue and remained one for close to ten years before it was removed.

With the constant battle with snowmobiles in the winter and ATVs in the summer, plowing the road became an issue. The Andersons were the only full-time residents. The rest of us were using our property as second homes. The Andersons would frequently call whichever plowing company the association had contracted with to complain about not plowing at the mandatory six inches of new snow, or for plowing too much.

At one point, the Andersons limited the width of the plowed road to effectively allow only one car width. That width is okay with a long driveway, but on a two-mile stretch of road that several homes use for access, it became an issue. The year Anderson did this, we had a large dumping of snow, close to two feet in a few days. Plowing that amount really isn't a problem, but with the shoulders already built up and iced over, there was nowhere for the snow to go. I had to call in a bulldozer to clear the downhill side. The road was impassable until I did this.

Instead of thanking me for clearing the road, Anderson immediately criticized me for damaging the road surface. I'm not a civil engineer by trade, but my father was, and I spent many summers working interstate highway construction. I understand how roads are built. Regardless, Anderson now decided he would not pay for clearing the snow. Since we were keeping the road wide and pushing snow off the side of the hill, he decided to place large boulders on the access road that passed through his property. This created an issue with the plowing company.

THE HOSTILE TAKEOVER

This Anderson nonsense went on for several years. Not being on the board, he finally understood that he couldn't really drive things the way he wanted and started to soften in some of his actions. We had several meetings with him, and he convinced the membership he was worthy of leading the association. After a discussion at a meeting, we elected him president of the HOA. From the start, it was obvious this was a mistake. He tried to run the association like a multi-million-dollar corporation and hired lawyers to provide evidence that we didn't understand how to run the association—only he did. At one point, I read the Revised Code of Washington that governed homeowners associations and went through each section and wrote commentary on each. After all, my opinion is just as valid as his lawyer's—only a judge could make a legal decision. (Anderson did not like me saying that, but it helped that my brother is an attorney.) We had not had an annual meeting for several years, and Anderson ran the organization like some kind of dictator. If he didn't like what you were doing, he would threaten to sue you. We also didn't elect new officers yearly as dictated by our governing documents. He was king. I'd finally had enough and organized a membership meeting to hold elections. Anderson said we were not operating per Washington State law, and once again threatened to sue us. When most of the association backed down, I resigned as a board member.

After the meeting, another member called and we discussed actions we could take. We contacted probably the most experienced trial and homeowners association attorney in Seattle and started our takeover. It was quite an education. We found out that we hadn't been running the association correctly at all over the ten or so years it had existed. She helped us get organized and up to speed with being within the law. Then, we set out to have a special membership meeting for removal of a board member as allowed by the governing document.

When the letter went out, Mr. Anderson formally quit his position and left all association matters to his wife. In the meeting that followed, we only had to vote for the new board. We also held a vote on a special assessment to get funding to pay for plowing and road maintenance. The meetings we held after this were actually fun. We ran them using Robert's Rules of Order to adhere to parliamentary procedure and documented everything very formally. At one point, the Andersons' lawyer was corrected by ours on finer points of homeowner law.

We had a budget and assessed all the properties. Everyone paid except for the Andersons. They decided our actions were not valid in their eyes. I think they had a fundamental issue with either not being in charge or being told what to do.

Remember the gate…well, nobody liked the gate. In a meeting with our lawyer, we discussed it and said we should hold a membership vote to remove it. Much to our surprise, the board, three of us out of the eight, could make that decision without a vote by the membership. We reaffirmed we were a homeowners association and served notice to remove the gate and the boulders on the roadway. If not, we would remove them at the Andersons' expense. This was an emotional issue and probably the one key thing the Andersons held sacred in the association. It was their gate—their statement of power and defiance—and they demanded it stay in place.

THE LAWSUIT(S)

As the amount owed—for non-payment of dues, costs for removal of gates and debris left on the association easement, legal obligations to the association, and interest in the outstanding amount—by the Andersons grew, we decided we needed to take action. We placed a lien on their property for the amount due, 18 percent APR, and legal fees. The amount was large, but manageable. It also included removal of their gate and boulders from the roadway. It was a watershed moment for the association.

The Andersons typically resolved issues involving money by suing people. This, though, was different—we had removed something sacred to them, and they wanted it restored. They countersued, claiming harassment from the association president, and they sued the association for medical claims from Mr. Anderson for allegedly being hurt while working on the easement. The amount specified in their lawsuit pretty much equaled our claim. They then demanded we enter into binding arbitration—effectively presenting both cases to an impartial person and being held to their decision. They even had someone in mind they had used in the past.

We said no.

They then went after the board for wasting association money in this lawsuit, and I think they were shocked when we informed them we had insurance that covered all the costs. Remember, we were operating the association by the book now, which included directors and association insurance.

I could write a lot about this case alone, including Mrs. Anderson's claims and legal briefs back and forth. In the end, they lost—and they lost big. By the time the court case was complete, the ruling stated that the Andersons owed around $60,000, had no jurisdiction on the easement (the gate would not go back up), and upon appeal, Mrs. Anderson needed to put up a bond for complete payment. No bond was posted, and we started a sheriff's sale to sell the Andersons' property to recoup our judgment. We were a week or two from the sale when COVID-19 hit, and it was put on hold. As of this writing, the COVID-19 holds by the court have been lifted and a sheriff's sale was completed to recoup the amount the association was owed, now in the six-digit range.

SUMMARY

Mrs. Anderson called me during the legal activities and asked why I was doing this—it must be costing me a lot. My response was, "This is no longer about money. It's about principle. What is going on here is not right, and I'm not going to stand for it anymore." I have so many stories about my experiences with the Andersons from threatening email from her to outlandish claims or accusations. One email was particularly hostile, and I drafted a similarly worded response. Before I sent it, I called my brother the lawyer and discussed it with him. He said, "Don't respond; that's what she wants." I didn't, and the next day it was apparent my lack of response bothered her even more.

What can we learn from this situation?

Do not engage hostility with hostility.

By not getting hostile with people and keeping an even keel, they become the owners of the hostility and people will recognize that. It can be hard sometimes, but not sending an email right away, or pausing before responding, can help, especially with difficult relationships.

Do not back down when bullied.

When I was growing up, a bully was someone who threatened physical harm. Today, bullying manifests in many different forms from cyber, legal, or harassment. When threatened by someone, defend yourself, and make it clear you will continue to do so. That, by itself, may avert the problem, and the bully may look for someone else to prey on.

Work on building relationships.

You never know when you may need someone's help. Mr. Anderson drove off the road one night while the plowing contractor was up there. Anderson asked for help. It would have been easy to help him, but Anderson had sued the contractor who pulled him out the year before for damages he claimed the plow driver caused. The last thing the plow contractor was going to do was provide assistance. But he did help by calling a tow truck, and after an hour or more and $300, Anderson was pulled out of the ditch. A relationship needs to be genuine and consistent, even if it's with someone who may be hostile.

EXERCISES

1. Have you sent a note you wish you could take back?

    _____

    _____

    _____

    _____

    _____

2. What are some strategies for interacting with hostile people?

_____

_____

_____

3. Describe a situation where you worked at building a relationship in-dependent of help you may need.

_____

_____

_____

CHAPTER 3

PEOPLE ARE WATCHING

"What you do has far greater impact than what you say."

— Stephen Covey

THE STORK HAS ARRIVED

I took a class in St. Louis at the Boeing Leadership Center. It was taught by a woman (let's call her Ms. Crowley) who was an expert on male-female relationships. In the class, Ms. Crowley highlighted the differences between men and women and described an experiment that showed how these differences start at birth.

Ms. Crowley had come in and walked all around the front of the room, putting her foot up on chairs that had been placed strategically. Then she started her presentation. After about fifteen minutes, she went behind a podium at the front of the room and asked, "Who can tell me what color my shoes are?" Not a male in the room had a clue, but all of the women did. When she came out from behind the podium, it was obvious the shoes didn't match what she was wearing and really stood out if you paid attention. I thought to myself, *Wow, those are really ugly shoes.*

Ms. Crowley then talked about an experiment held at the university where she taught. In the experiment, they placed an employment ad and selected an equal number of men and women to interview. Prior to the interview, each candidate was asked to sit in a very cluttered room and wait for thirty minutes. The interviewers then collected the candidate, took them to another room, and asked them to describe what was in the room where they had spent thirty minutes. The men could only describe a few items, while the women listed a much larger number.

Another experiment took a newborn child and dressed them in all the cultural dress and colors of little girls. They handed the child to a couple and asked them to interact with the child. They then took the child, dressed it up in what are thought of as boy's clothes (the same child) and handed it back to the couple to interact with. When the couple was holding the "girl," they placed "her" on their laps facing themselves. During the session, noises were introduced, and the experiment was all about face-to-face interaction with the child. The "boy," on the other hand, was placed on the lap but faced outward. When a noise was introduced, the couple commented on the child's external environment.

Ms. Crowley's point was men and women are different genetically, and we make them even more different culturally from birth. As a boy, you grow up, get into a pecking order with your peers, and, based on your position, know what is expected of you. Life is good. This is probably true for those with a different gender identity.

As a girl, there isn't a pecking order; there are cliques where the members of the clique are equal. The cliques, though, are not equal, and as an adolescent, there can be a lot of movement between cliques, causing stress on girls. Since I'm the father of two girls, Ms. Crowley suggested I get my girls grounded in a sport or other activity outside of school to help mitigate the negative aspects of cliques.

After this training, I went back to work, but I noticed that when women talk with each other, it is face to face and the external environment is effectively ignored. Men, on the other hand, interact with the external environment while communicating. This came front and center when a new female employee walked into my office. She asked if we could talk, and I said sure. At the time, the engineering workforce was primarily men, and as a manager, I'd had many requests for such meetings in the past. I started to talk to her, but then turned around to complete an email. When I turned around, she was gone.

The lesson I'd learned from Ms. Crowley had not taken hold—my female employee was expecting my focus to be on the discussion with her. I went to talk to her, apologized, and explained she would probably run into this type of behavior again, but from that point on, whenever anyone came in to talk to me, man or woman, I dropped everything, moved away from my desk, and made it clear they had my full attention. After all, it's only common courtesy.

I bring these stories up to highlight that from birth, we are conditioned to behave in a certain manner, and we are watched to see if we are acting appropriately. Understanding these differences and taking them beyond gender to ethnicity highlights how we all have cultural differences that make us unique. Even if we look alike, we could come from different parts of the world where the cultural norms are very different. Understanding this and learning to operate in this diverse environment is critical for success in today's world.

THE SCHOOLYARD

My second daughter, Danielle, was born in early June. Because of her birthdate, she made the cut-off for going to school early, making her almost a year younger than most of the kids in her class. If we held her back, she would be one of the older children in her class. Probably the biggest mistake we made with her was sending her to school early. We didn't think much of the age difference since Danielle was a very outgoing girl and could sit down and talk to adults at length. What could be the problem with sending her early?

Developing children have distinct maturity levels from grade to grade. Soon after Danielle entered second grade, she told us she didn't want to go to school anymore, saying many of her classmates made fun of her and made her cry. When she cried, she was made fun of even more. As this went on, even her close friends started to distance themselves to avoid being made fun of for being her friend. When we met with the school counselor, she commented that this was a common issue with children who are younger than their classmates and not as mature as the older kids. I was heartbroken. What had we done?

Danielle, my wife, and I met with a counselor, and Danielle also met with her alone. After Danielle was aware of what was going on and how to handle it, her friends came back, and the teasing essentially went away. When you don't get an expected reaction, you move on to something else. We sat down with Danielle and helped her cope with the problem. We said it would probably go on for a few years until the maturity of all her classmates leveled off. To limit the teasing, she needed to hold in her tears and not lash out. If she felt like crying, she should do it privately. It worked, but it changed her. Danielle became reserved for many years, afraid to expose herself to ridicule.

If I had to do this again, my advice to other parents would be to hold the child back before they start school. This will allow them to mature and, hopefully, address one of many challenges they will face growing up.

GOING TO WORK

My most significant life change was probably my first day of work and first month working. Going to college was more of going to high school, just with no parents, off on your own. Those who didn't have the good fortune of going to college probably missed what I think is the best transition from adolescence to adulthood. You were on your own in a protected environment. The friends you met in college often became lifelong friends. I did not enter the military, but I think the same can be said for that experience.

On my first day of work, I didn't have anyone really helping me get to work or find the office I needed to report to. I started work at the Boeing Company in Renton, Washington. The Renton site was where the 727, 737, and 757 were then being built and tens of thousands of employees were on site. I had instructions about where to go, but it was overwhelming. I finally found where I needed to report, met with my boss, and sat down at my desk. I was the new, fresh-out-of-college employee, and the engineers really didn't know what to do with me, so they did what we still do today—gave me a mountain of documents to read.

My first week was really depressing. I thought work would be eight hours of homework for the rest of my life with endless documents to read and make sense of. As I began to lose hope, my lead showed up; he'd been on vacation, but now sat me down to get to know me. We really didn't talk about work. We talked about our exploits in college, where I grew up, and what interested me. At the time, I didn't pay much attention to what he was really doing, but he was effectively testing me and trying to understand how I communicated, how comfortable I was in my new surroundings, and setting up a rapport with me that would last until he left the company.

That's when I really got excited because I understood work would not be non-stop homework, but challenging tasks and cool things to work on. One of the first things we did was tour the factory and then visit the labs. This wasn't a college lab with parts and tests that had been run for decades with the multitude of students who had passed through—this was real stuff that went onto airplanes that had to work and work safely.

They gave me tasks, but I completed them quickly and soon ran out of things to work on, so I took some initiative and got an account on the Digital Equipment Corporation VAX mainframe computer. I even got an account on the CRAY supercomputer that Boeing had. The CRAY, at the time, was the most powerful computer in the world and was used for aerodynamic modeling of airplanes at Boeing.

One day, my lead asked why I had the accounts. He told me he was aware and watching to see what I was doing. What I was doing was modeling the fire detection system for the 757 airplane, and I had a pretty robust computer model for it. This single act actually gave me a head start over all the other new college graduates and ownership of a system on the airplane.

As my career progressed, I soon became aware that how you acted in meetings was very important and how you answered questions was equally important. An engineer asking why a valve didn't close expected a technical response. An executive just wanted to know you had a fix for it. As you worked on problems on the new airplanes you were developing, how you communicated issues and how you carried yourself would get you invited into the big meetings instead of getting information secondhand. By being in the big meetings, you were visible and those with influence on your career took notice.

I was cornered in a meeting once while presenting technical data. The chief engineer started asking detailed questions, and I was quickly over my head, losing the message I was trying to convey. I was very frustrated by the exchange and didn't do a good job trying to communicate the message. When I asked my boss what I had done wrong, he explained that, as an engineer first, the chief still liked to engineer the problem. My mistake was putting data into the presentation instead of focusing on the message. Chief engineers don't get many opportunities to get into technical detail, and by adding data to the presentation, I had opened the door for a technical exchange I was not prepared for.

MANAGEMENT

I truly enjoyed my job. Like all jobs, there are good days and bad days, but I got to work on these amazing machines that flew people all over the world. As I told people when I retired, it was a true privilege to be a part of bringing people together all over the world. We live in a unique time in history. In just over the last 100 years, we have flown, reached the moon, and seen technological changes only dreamt of before, and witnessed the world transform from an industrial to an information and then a persuasion economy. Several hundred years from now, people will look back at this age and comment that this is where it all began.

These are also very unique times—times I don't think many appreciate or even contemplate. We have looked to the skies for centuries and thought of flying. As comedian Louis CK said on *Late Night with Conan O'Brien* in 2012, "Everything is amazing right now, and nobody is happy…it is wasted on the crappiest generation of just spoiled idiots." He then discussed passengers on airplanes, stating, "They act as if their flight was a cattle car in the '40s in Germany…[the flight] was the worst day of my life." Then he said, "Everyone on a flight should say, 'Oh, my God, wow'… you're sitting in a chair in the sky!"

The advances we have made in both technology and aviation are nothing short of amazing. I was lucky enough to be part of both for more than thirty years. I worked in a small fraternity called aviation where you ran across the same people, just in different positions or in different companies. When I hadn't seen someone in a while, the first thing I'd ask was where they worked now.

I spent significant time overseas working and understanding different cultures, and I got insights into and an up-close-and-personal view of large commercial aircraft. One of many highlights in my career was a private tour of the Concord before it was retired and many flights in the cockpit of a 747 during takeoff and landing. Few people can claim to have done those cool things.

In my engineering job, after a few years, I started thinking of where I really wanted to end up. I was doing and working on really interesting and significant things, but it was always someone else's idea or design. After some thought and discussion, I decided management was the path for me. I came to this decision by consulting folks with different perspectives, something I would counsel employees approaching the same decision to do.

For me, the process looked like this. First, I didn't really like the decisions my bosses were making. Second, I didn't really want to dive deeply into the technical side, especially with airplane technology starting to evolve at the speed of consumer electronics. I decided management was for me. I did go into it with my eyes open, though. I understood that as I moved up the food chain, the number of people I could really have a deep relationship with would get even smaller. I also understood many people who had been critical of me would suddenly become my friends, at least to my face. After all, I would have the power to influence their jobs, salary, and working conditions.

Making the decision, I pressed forward. I made my career aspirations clear to management and worked to start looking at things from a bigger perspective. I always had an ability to see beyond the immediate, and I started to show this to those who could help me. I started presenting in review meetings and asked for feedback on my performance, and I often got direct feedback in the meeting—usually feedback critical of what and how I presented. I was okay, though; this was new ground and I needed to learn. At year five, I was given a lead position and appointed to represent the Federal Aviation Administration as a Designated Engineering Representative in showing our design compliance to regulations. I also took the test offered by the State of Washington to become a professional engineer. I was on my way.

About year six, I moved to cabin systems. I didn't know it at the time, but thirty years later, I'd retire from essentially the same group, although the group ended up working on much more than the small video systems in the 1990s. At my retirement, these systems were some of the most complex systems on the airplane.

I applied for a management job, and after an elaborate process, got it. The candidates took a written test in which we navigated certain scenarios, roleplayed a mock employee interaction, and took a timed test in which we prioritized the test items in order to complete the test on time. Being an engineer, I knew there had to be some objective way to score all of this, and so, for the written test, I had my wife Bonnie read my answers. If she understood what I said and it related to the question, human resources or management would understand it.

Bonnie pointed out one question I hadn't really answered: Discuss a mistake you've made. My wife, of course, was right, so I documented a big mistake I had made in my second year at Boeing. The error would have had significant consequences, but more on that later.

For the roleplay, we received vague instructions, so I asked, "If you didn't list something as a condition, can I ad-lib?" I was told yes. My scenario was a disgruntled employee whom I was supposed to counsel about his concerns based on rumors that everyone was getting laid off. I guess I was supposed to follow that line of thought, but that wasn't a ground rule. I told him we had just won several new projects and would actually be hiring. I saw the moderator was not thrilled with this ad lib—it was not what they intended.

I'm not sure what happened after that, but I passed all the steps and got the job. Later, someone complained about the process, and Boeing made the course creators take the tests. That was the last time the process was used. I guess they didn't do very well.

I was then a full-fledged manager. I got the secret manager meeting notices, got all my group's payroll information, and was given an evaluation on one of my new employees who was not doing well.

I actually got to go to what I called the "secret managers' meeting," and after attending, I understood why it was good that the employees didn't know what happened in them. The managers had their own issues that often trumped the stuff on the floor, and they had no real plan to address much of it.

All of the leads then stopped by either to tell me I was a genius or test me. Since I was new to management, people realized I had just left the ranks of the working class and understood their needs and desires. The people under me asked for all sorts of things, from working virtually to getting them wireless cards and pagers (a perk at the time). I'm not sure I actually had the authority to get them, but it became obvious their motives were not pure—they were going to take advantage of my new position before I got wise. Many new managers have experienced this. My advice on dealing with it is to just say no or tell them you'll talk to a more experienced manager. This usually ended the ridiculous requests portion of the new manager ritual.

Managing a group of employees is kind of like raising children. They test you. They ask the same question over and over again and have multiple people do so. I know because I used to do the same thing to my manager. We figured if we asked enough, sooner or later we'd get the answer we wanted—kind of like asking Mom and then Dad. The best example of this was when we combined two groups that were working on different electronic features on the seats (power ports, inflight entertainment, emergency lighting, and motorized features for business and first-class seats) into one group.

Historically, as two groups, each would send an engineer to the supplier, often in a picturesque country, to evaluate the facilities. I called many of these trips and the people who took them "the travel club." When we combined the groups, the two travel club members still wanted to go. One of the best things I did in this situation is still talked about today. They both came into my office with travel requests. I told them only one could go, and they needed to decide who it would be. They left and came back shortly claiming they both still needed to go. Throwing both travel requests on my desk, they waited for my response.

I took the one that landed on top, picked it up slowly, looked them both in the eyes without even looking at the request, and tore it in half. They were both frantically trying to see which one I had torn up when I picked up the second, crossed the name off of it, and wrote someone else's in its place. I chose someone I knew they both would not approve of and told them, "Thanks. If you can't make a decision, I will." They took the paper back and said they would figure it out. They knew I was serious and would have sent someone else. That is the last time I had that kind of discussion with anyone in the group, and the story traveled to other groups I managed over time.

The other classic thing I did that is still talked about is when an employee came in to complain about something like parking that no one in the company really had any influence over. As a manager, it is your job to listen to this kind of stuff and let people vent or get mundane things off their chest. This discussion just wouldn't stop, though. I started playing with a pencil. I dropped it, and it fell on the floor. When I bent down to pick it up, the employee asked what I was doing. I told him I was looking for my violin, to which he replied that I didn't have to be such an asshole. I'm not sure what made me say it or how I thought of it at the time. It was actually brilliant, though. He figured out he had gone on too long, and after that, others in the group would tell people when they complained, "Be careful, or John will go get his violin," bringing an element of levity into the discussion.

THE FIVE FORMS OF POWER

I actually really enjoyed managing people, and I understood quickly that I was in a position to influence their career and success going forward, which created a unique opportunity if you could recognize it. While you were formally in charge of the group, you would sometimes get the feeling that people didn't listen or follow your direction. You also saw it in managers whom people had problems with. One key to successful leadership is letting go and delegating the work to others. This is often hard for new managers and experienced ones who came up through the ranks. I learned this as a lead with one of my engineers. I was telling him how to accomplish a task when he asked me to leave him alone for a week. I did, waiting for the end of the week before I set him straight. When we sat down and he showed me what he had done, it was apparent that *I* hadn't understood the task. He had, and he actually did a much better job than I would have if I had followed my initial thoughts. Delegating is important. And after, you have to support your employees no matter the result.

As a newly minted manager, I decided to get my master's degree in business administration (MBA). It was something I believed would help me rise to my highest level. (Later I found it didn't really matter.) During one of the courses, the instructor introduced the "five forms of power," first created by social psychologists John French and Bertram Raven in 1959. The five forms of power are:

1. Coercive Power

2. Reward Power

3. Legitimate Power

4. Referent Power

5. Expert Power

Most of those should be somewhat self-explanatory based on their names, except perhaps referent power. It may also be intuitive how one might move from one form to another over time. Since I was formally in charge of the group, I had legitimate power, the weakest form of power. But let's look at referent power for a moment.

Referent is the strongest form of power. Sitting in a group, if you pay attention, you can often spot who is really driving the discussion. The boss may be upfront in giving direction, but the group is often looking at one individual whom they will ultimately align with. This could best be described by looking at the relationship between a bright first lieutenant and the first sergeant in a platoon. The officer has legitimate power, but often the first sergeant has more experience and commands more respect, thereby having more influence over the platoon. One of my colleagues was a first lieutenant in Vietnam and understood this. He made an arrangement with the first sergeant to manage the platoon with him, thus keeping the men in line with the lieutenant and keeping the brass off everyone's back.

You can't pick which form of power you want. Getting promoted gets you legitimate power, where you can also exert coercive or reward power, but expert or referent power require much more interaction and knowledge of the group and subject matter. You need to understand where you are, understand where the expert and referent power are in your group, and leverage that power until you can move into that position. The most powerful thing you can do as a manager is keep up the morale of the group, convince them you have a plan, and make them feel you will you have their backs when things go wrong. I got my expert power as an engineer on the flight line when I helped a technician solve a problem he was under pressure to solve. I gave him the credit, but he remembered, and he told all the other flight line folks that I knew what I was doing.

PEOPLE ARE WATCHING

Hopefully, you've gathered that leading a group is not just sending out orders and hoping everyone will obey. First, you often don't know what the orders should be, and second, you may not be the right person to define the orders. The people doing the work are. People are always watching. Once when I had a female employee come into my office, rumors of some funny business started. I was alerted of the rumors by my office administrator. (Always have someone in the group whom people will use to send you messages.) I understood and took action to ensure my interactions were transparent and honorable. Probably the best compliment I ever got was something I overheard from an employee during a time when the company was downsizing. He was asked by another if he was worried about getting laid off. He said, "No, John doesn't seem worried, so neither am I." Now, the downsizing was real, but I had a handle on it and didn't make it a public issue. That day I realized how much my personality had migrated into the group and how they followed my lead. If we overran some budget, if I didn't take issue with it, neither did the group. On a couple of occasions, I made it known that we needed to step it up and the group responded. In later chapters, I'll give more examples that highlight this key principle and how it works with other principles.

SUMMARY

Research suggests it only takes seven seconds for others to form a solid impression of who you are. If you are interviewing for a job, often the decision whether to hire you is made in the time it takes to walk you to the interview room. When you board an airplane, a flight attendant is sizing you up to see if you may be a problem or someone they can reach out to in an emergency.

Flight attendants are also starting to be trained to recognize people trafficking in humans. I have talked to one who recognized a couple with a son where the situation didn't seem right. Using some techniques they'd been trained on, they were able to identify the situation, alert the captain, and have authorities waiting at the airport. When you arrive to check into an airport in Israel, the gate agent gives you a risk factor based on their training and your behavior. This rating follows you to the plane as you proceed through security and final boarding checks.

At work in a leadership position, people are watching. Your group is watching to see if you have a plan, and your bosses are watching to see if you have a "command presence" in meetings and reviews.

What lessons can be taken from this?

Diversity is much deeper than what you see.

Men and women are different physically and culturally, but their differences can be much broader than this. A person's background, culture, and religious upbringing all build their unique perspective on the world and how they interact with it and solve problems. It is critical to recognize this and leverage it. By getting diverse perspectives, you will be much more successful and have a group that is engaged and empowered.

Understanding where people are from a developmental perspective is critical.

The example I provided earlier relates to my daughter, but the same is true your entire life. You need to understand where people are in their understanding of work, the job, experience in the technology, and maturity in working with people. In my MBA curriculum, I had a mentor from a local TV station. He said that half my job was making sure people are in positions they can succeed at. The other half is the responsibility of the person working. If they fail, you bear a big part of the failure. You put them in a position they were not prepared for.

Over time, more people are watching you.

In school, many people may be watching, but typically, just your immediate friends. As you transition to work, your teammates and others you work with are watching and evaluating what kind of person you are and if you can help them. Moving into management and potentially senior management, you are much more visible and more people know who you are. I will often run across someone at work who says hi to me by name. It often takes me a moment to remember their name. As an executive, expectations about my behavior were much higher than when I was a new hire engineer because of my visibility and potential to embarrass the company. When I retired, I was well known both within the company and in many industry and government circles. The last thing I wanted was behavior that would tarnish my reputation and my career success.

Understanding the sources of power is critical.

Knowing where the power is in an organization, both in management and in your local group, is critical. Do you know whom you need to work with before bringing an idea forward? Meeting with an influential leader and getting buy-in on an idea can be the difference between success and failure. When you involve a leader, they get recognition for the idea and you gain support publicly, thus increasing your influence. Within your group, the same is true. I had technical fellows in my group who were scary smart. By working on ideas with them, I had a better product and something with technical backing from the people who would be expected to do the work and make to project succeed.

EXERCISES

1. Pay attention to male-male and female-female discussions. Do you notice a difference in how they communicate?

    _____

    _____

    _____

    _____

    _____

    _____

2. Have you done things with people that got positive responses? Negative ones?

_____

_____

_____

_____

_____

3. Who in your workgroup, club, or group really has the power?

_____

_____

_____

_____

_____

CHAPTER 4

DOING THE RIGHT THING

"You only live once, but if you do it right, once is enough."

— Mae West

THE WEDNESDAY NIGHTER

I've said it earlier and will probably repeat it many times in this book—growing up in Montana in the 1970s and 1980s was probably the best time and place to grow up. There was a sense of fairness and tolerance for young adults to test the waters. We learned early that there was a line, a gray area, and a cliff you didn't wander off. If you were driving fast, drinking underage, or committing some other minor offense, you admitted it to the authorities, often the police. We, all my friends and I, followed a code (although that was often gray as well): never damage private property and don't hurt anyone. We learned early that tolerance came with some common courtesy. Property owners would turn a blind eye if you left everything as it was when you arrived. I kind of knew it as I entered puberty and started driving, but a couple of events firmly cemented it in.

When I grew up, the drinking age was eighteen, meaning most high school seniors could drink legally. Also at the time, drinking and driving was not as serious of an offense as it is now. Mothers Against Drunk Driving was formed when I was in college, and when I was in high school, you really had to work hard to get a DUI. Getting pulled over for a traffic offense wasn't something you really worried about.

I do need to clarify something here before we go further. I do not condone drinking and driving, and I believe society has really changed these behaviors in a good way. My daughters would not think of doing it, but it was the reality growing up at that time.

If the circumstances warranted, the police would ask if you'd been drinking, and most drivers would answer yes. (Remember, don't lie to the police.) They would either escort you home, have someone else in the car drive you home, or instruct you to go straight home.

The bottom line is seniors could legally drink in high school until I became a senior. When I became a senior, they changed the drinking age to nineteen, but it didn't really change anything. What it did was push us out of public spaces to private ones, a farmer's field or the railroad track right of way.

The Wednesday Nighter was a weekly event where everyone chipped in on a keg of beer and drove twenty to thirty miles out of town to drink it. We would meet by the railroad tracks, start a fire, and have a beer. The location was not widely known, and those who stumbled on it by accident were encouraged to leave. It was actually a fun event, and at our ten-year reunion, the original sponsors hosted one again for old times' sake.

This event was unique because all different social classes would attend: jocks, freaks, and some nerds. (I'm not sure which one I was, but I was invited.) We would clean up all the garbage, put the fire out, and leave the place pretty much as it was, except the burned-out firepit.

The railroad used the space frequently. They had a gate, but never locked it, and we'd see at times that someone else had started a fire in the same place, but there was never any garbage. It was too good of a thing to mess up.

Many weeks into the school year, on a night when I couldn't make it to the party, the guy who normally brought firewood didn't show up and they had to scavenge wood. In eastern Montana, we didn't have a lot of nice firewood laying around, especially near railroad tracks. In any case, something was found to get a fire started—some old railroad ties. The railroad was upgrading the roadbed and replacing railroad ties, leaving the old ones behind. They kind of looked like firewood, just bigger, and when put on the small fire, they took right off, so more were put on. Pretty soon, we had a fire nobody was going to be able to put out.

Railroad ties are soaked in creosote, which helps preserve them. Now, creosote is flammable and in a hot fire, it will burn hot and leave a large black cloud of smoke behind. It is also exceedingly difficult to put out once it starts, at least for high school students. The fire department had to be called. Since I wasn't there, I don't know exactly how it ended, but the railroad had had enough. They locked the gate and made sure nobody accessed that area or others like it.

When I transitioned from high school to college, most of my friends went with me. Moving into college gave us freedom we didn't have while at home, but it didn't really change the drinking. One night, it happened to me. I was driving fifty in a thirty-five zone at 1:00 a.m. when I passed a police car and got pulled over. Now, being in college and in a fraternity, many of my brothers had been pulled over for DUI and gone to a court-mandated school. They learned you can smell the alcohol on someone's breath and tell if their speech is slurred (along with other miscellaneous facts). I knew this, so I rolled my windows down, told my passenger not to open his mouth, and when the police officer approached my car, I gave him my license and nodded when he told me he was going to cite me for speeding. He went to his cruiser, and when he came back, he asked for my phone number—which I couldn't recall.

My friend let out a belly laugh when the officer asked if I'd been drinking. I said, "Yes." I think he was a little shocked, but he told me, "See that stop sign? After that, you are no longer my responsibility." In Montana at the time, jurisdiction was honored, meaning if you were driving fast and passed a sheriff from another county, they could not pull you over. This is not true now, at least in Washington State.

SNOWBANKS AND FOUR-WHEEL DRIVES

Growing up in an area with four seasons included the adventure of learning to drive in snow and how to have some fun doing it. Learning to drive in snow is not something you can read about or watch on YouTube. You have to experience it. Every car has a unique feel to it, but once you understand the basics, you are set for most situations.

The basics—drive fast going uphill, slow going down. The slow going down is obvious, but going uphill isn't as intuitive. It just takes one trip up a hill going too slow and hitting an icy patch for your car to lose forward momentum and leave you stuck. To get unstuck, you have to back down the hill, which in case you are wondering, is no fun at all.

When I was growing up, cars were transitioning from mostly rear wheel drive to front wheel drive. The front wheel drive really made driving in snow much easier—and it also helped you learn new maneuvers, like backing up and pulling the emergency brake, locking up the rear wheels. It was kind of a cut-rate Rockford turn without the horsepower of a Firebird. (Watch *The Rockford Files* to understand a Rockford turn.)

Funny now how everyone has to have an all-wheel drive to navigate a snowy road with some even chaining up for no apparent reason. We only put chains on if we were stuck, and then we immediately took them off. (The way our society and technology are moving, there will be only a handful who can actually drive on snowy roads in the not-so-distant future.) On one trip, I installed them and removed them three times. My father didn't even believe in putting chains on. This was also a time when radial tires were coming on the market, and he commented that a good set of radials were just as good as chaining up. If he did have chains in the car (as required when going over mountain passes), chances are they didn't fit. From Dad's perspective, he met the letter of the law. I don't know if he ever actually chained his car up, but if he did, he would never admit it publicly.

We had a Buick Electra—probably the largest car Buick made at the time. It had a 455 cubic inch, big block engine, and the interior held six to eight, depending on how cozy you wanted to get. The trunk was big enough to hold five bodies. I know that because when we went skiing one day, we were informed that chains were required. That is how I found out my dad didn't have the right size chains and that just having chains in the car was good enough—they didn't need to fit. We decided to go for it without chains. After all, the car had radial tires—they're just as good.

About halfway up the hill, we started to lose momentum and were coming to a stop. I popped the trunk and told the other five passengers to get out and push. When we started moving, they jumped into the trunk. We had to do this a couple of more times to get to the top of Red Lodge Mountain. My father was right—and it was much easier to have the folks in your car jump out to give you a push than lay on your back in the snow putting chains on.

As I moved on from high school to college, I had several cars from a front wheel drive Honda Prelude to a Chevy Camaro Rally Sport and a Jeep Cherokee Chief. They all had their unique aspects, but the Camaro really drove the best in light snow, so long as you didn't have to stop or slow down. It had a low center of gravity and much better handling package than the small Honda or the Jeep. That said, the Jeep was a fun vehicle to have. It allowed me to cross rivers, although I chickened out my first time when the guy in front of me stalled and got swept down the Madison River. In the snow, it was good and would go through anything. I never got stuck and would often pull people out of ditches. At speed, though, it didn't handle as well as the Camaro.

One very snowy night we were driving around Bozeman on the campus of Montana State University in my Jeep. We were heading to North Hedges and could see it in the distance, but we had to navigate snow-covered roads to get there. Coming to a stop, we faced what was probably a three- to four-foot berm of fresh snow. The roads had just been plowed after a good snowstorm. There it was, the berm, probably 200 yards of a fresh snowy field, and another berm to get back onto the road. We decided to go for it—there is nothing like crashing through snow, having it fly over your windshield, and then crashing through another berm of snow.

Upon reaching the end of the field, we noticed we had another field to go to get to North Hedges. I put the pedal to the metal, and off we went into the second field. We pulled up on the road at the entrance of the dormitory and my friend went in to get something. I got out of the car and marveled at my accomplishment. You could clearly see my path with a snowy trail following my Jeep. Right then, a campus cop pulled up with his light on. Turns out he was right behind me, but he couldn't follow us off road. He got out of the car and asked me, "Did you just do that?" Looking back, it was pretty obvious, so I said yes.

"Why did you do that?"

I pondered for a moment and replied, "Look at it. How could you resist?"

He looked at it for a moment, then said, "You know what, I'm going to pretend this didn't happen because you were truthful," and we talked a little about driving four-wheel drives in the snow. Right then, his partner showed up. Turns out he had got out of the car when he saw me stop and followed me on foot through my snowy path. Needless to say, he wasn't happy his partner let me go.

FARM BOYS

Many of my cousins worked on farms and ranches. I spent a summer at one of their ranches and spent time at my uncle's farm in Minnesota. The one truth is farmers and ranchers are probably some of the hardest working people I've met, and that follows them their entire life. After these experiences, I decided college was good—working on a farm was a lot of work.

I would often hear stories about my cousins rolling pickups after working long days during the harvest season when my mother was talking to her sister on the phone. One of my cousins still has a pickup his grandfather, father, and he each rolled. I think that family tradition is finally broken, but he looks at the truck as a family heirloom and has plans to refurbish it.

After a long night when my cousins were younger, my cousin Danny came home late. In pulling into the farm, he took a corner too wide and hit his brother's parked car. Now, the driveway was wide to accommodate large farm machinery between the house and barn. There was lots of room for vehicles. Not knowing what to do, he pulled his car around one of the machine sheds and parked it for the night. That next morning, my uncle got up and noticed Peter's car was damaged. Now, Peter had come home late as well and didn't quite remember whether he had gotten into an accident or not, but his dad was not happy and started to quiz him at high volume about what had happened. Peter didn't know how to respond. After listening a bit to the words between Peter and his dad, Danny decided to come clean—and also suffered his father's wrath. (My uncle could weave a "tapestry of obscenity," just like that mentioned in the movie *A Christmas Story*, and I'm sure it wasn't pleasant being on the receiving side of the discussion.)

Following this, my uncle's neighbors would come over and comment that he should get better lighting between the house and barn, which re-opened this scar. Later at Danny's wedding when I heard the story (along with Danny's new bride), I commented that his brother Dale wasn't a good brother—he had never rolled a pickup like the rest of them. If there is a lesson here, it is that the truth will always come out so it's often better to come out with it up front.

747s AND TURBINE OVERHEAT

Once out of college, my antics were a thing of the past (at least most of them). I was in the workplace and working at the Boeing Company. Growing up in Montana, I spent time on my uncles' ranches and farms. I had been around large machinery and marveled at the complexity and size of them. Even now, driving in southeastern Washington, I'll come across a farm implement store and the size of the equipment will still amaze me. Most are computer-operated now with GPS and sensors controlling how much fertilizer or seed to put out.

I was recruited into the electrical subsystems division starting with an airplane called the 7J7 (airplanes in development are given these types of designators). When I hired in, the 727 was still in production and the 7J7 was being designed to replace it. It had a similar shape but with two engines instead of three on the rear of the airplane. The unique part of the airplane was that the engines were un-ducted fans. These engines were like no others produced at the time. They looked like a jet engine turned backward without a cowling with the jet fan blades spinning on the rear of the engine. Kind of like a propeller engine turned backwards, but with a large set of fan blades rather than a propeller on the rear. I worked on this program for about six months, then volunteered to work on the 747 program in development. The 747 was being updated from a three-person flight deck (pilot, co-pilot, and flight engineer) to a two-person crew with just a pilot and co-pilot and updated avionics and systems. I had never seen a 747 or anything of that size before I really wanted to work on it.

When I arrived in Everett, Washington, where the 747 is built, I was in awe. The doors to the factory were the size of a football field. The airplane itself was 211 feet wide, 230 feet long, and sixty-three feet tall (six to seven stories). This plane was massive. It had four engines that developed 56,000 pounds of thrust, and as it turns out, it was the fastest commercial jet airliner in service.

I was put in charge of fire detection. Remember, I wrote a computer simulation for fire detection? Turns out people were watching. Fire detection is an essential system on an airplane and on Rolls Royce engines. The system has two sets of sensors in the engine: one to detect turbine overheat and one to detect engine fires. When triggered, the sensors issue an alert to the flight crew. While each engine has two independent systems, the alarm was the same in the flight deck. When the alarm sounded, a crew member pulled the corresponding engine fire handle, waited to see if the fire went out, then twisted the handle one way or the other to fire one of two extinguisher bottles. By pulling the fire handle, you stopped the fuel flow to the engine, isolated it electrically, and closed air bleed valves to isolate the engine and fire from the airplane. The system includes a test feature where you depress a switch in the flight deck, and it simulates an alarm, so you can validate that the system and associated indications are operating correctly. I was in charge of this system, probably only nine months after college. It was quite an accomplishment.

I understood the fire detection system on the 747 airplane intimately and went about defining the wiring and system installation aspects for it. This included wiring from the engine sensors to the controller in the electronics bay and wiring to the flight deck switches and indicators. An important part of the system was the test switch, and I defined the wiring from the controller as well. The airplane was built and my design installed. Then it was time to functionally test it (ensure it was wired correctly per the drawings). We would publish a formal Functional Test document and run the test in the factory. This is done on all the systems on the airplanes. Once all the tests passed, the airplane was ready for flight test and delivery. For this first airplane with this system, it was two weeks from delivery. This was the first 747 with turbine overheat detection installed.

One evening while driving home, I was thinking about how the system differed from other engines without turbine overheat. I remember the exact place on Interstate 5 where it dawned on me that I had made a critical mistake. How could I have been so stupid? I remember driving past an overpass and thinking that if I swerved into it, I wouldn't have to deal with this big mistake. It was a huge issue for me. I did know what to do. Maybe I could say nothing and act surprised when someone found the error—I knew someone would find it.

What I had done was wire both engine fire test sensors to both the engine fire detection system and the turbine overheat system. Since both had the same flight deck alert, a latent failure in one could go unnoticed. If I didn't fix it before we delivered the airplane, there would be issues with in-service airplanes and potential groundings while the fix was put in place.

I didn't sleep that night. I told myself I had to alert my management. If something happened to an airplane while in service, I couldn't have it weighing on my mind. The next day, I went in, told my manager, and expected to get fired. To my surprise, he understood it immediately, got some of the more senior engineers together, and we discussed the fix. Since I'd had all night to think about it, I knew what the fix was, but it was amazing to see the Boeing company taking action to address this safety issue. And I was never once criticized for the initial error. I was thanked for coming forward. We addressed the problem on the first delivery. At that moment, I was truly proud to be associated with the organization. I now understood the "safety culture" in aviation.

PROBLEMS ON THE FLIGHT LINE

I spent a lot of time on the flight line where the airplanes were parked after leaving the factory. Working in the design group, we were the frontline to the factory and the last stop for detecting and fixing in-service issues. Like anything in life, things happen, and part of our design and test process is to find the issues. As a manager, my group also spent a lot of time working on issues and testing new systems in the factory and flight line.

When you become a manager, you are suddenly responsible for a group of employees, some of whom you may be intimidated by. I was no different and ended up with Tom Smith. Tom was an ex-recon sniper who had served in Vietnam. He was a large, intimidating man. He made it clear he didn't appreciate how his abilities were being underappreciated. I thought about how I would work with Tom and decided just to engage him and see where things went. If he got upset that his raise wasn't large enough or people were getting better assignments, I'd deal with that in the moment. I had no idea what might come up or what my strategy would be.

By taking this tack, I soon found Tom really was an easy guy to get along with. All he wanted was to be treated fairly and with honesty, so that is how I interacted with him.

People would often ask me about metrics and how I measured success. I was never any good at those things and had people to do it for me. The one metric I paid attention to was how often Paul Vougt called me. Paul was the chief of the flight line and someone the customers and flight line personnel contacted first. Getting a call from Paul wasn't good. No calls from Paul meant things were going well. One call a week, not bad. Daily, you have issues and a daily discussion with him. One afternoon, Paul was quite upset when he called. One of my employees had done something stupid on an airplane. Paul wasn't sure who it was and asked me if I knew. I immediately said, "It was Tom. I'll check into it."

About thirty minutes later, Tom stopped by my desk, very agitated, and asked, "Did you say I did this on the flight line?" How could he know? How did he find out? We all face moments like this and have a decision to make. Do we deny it or tell the truth? I replied, "Yes, I did say you did it." "Why?" he asked. "Well," I said, "because when that happens on the flight line, you are the one who usually does it." He sat back, smiled, and said, "Thanks for being honest with me, but I didn't do it this time." After that, he truly became the easiest person to work with. He wanted respect and for you to be direct and truthful. That formula is not right for everyone, but for Tom it was.

SUMMARY

What did we learn here? When we work with people, we are daily challenged by how to respond to each situation. Not every situation requires a detailed answer, and some things can't be repeated, but we don't need to mask them. One of my old bosses used to say, "You cannot manage a secret, and the truth will set you free."

My father worked construction and once shared a story about his boss asking him to fire one of the superintendents who worked for his company. It was December 23, and the person was working on the interstate highway project in western Montana—about 430 miles west of our home. My father said okay, he'd take care of it after Christmas. His boss said, "Either you fire him today, or I'll replace you with someone who will."

I think my dad's boss expected my dad to call the guy to give him the bad news. The normal process would have been to call the person (if remote) and follow up by sending a severance check. My father didn't think firing the guy over the phone two days before Christmas and then mailing a check was right and decided on a different course of action. Dad got the guy's severance pay in cash, got into his car, and drove six-plus hours to tell him in person. He actually spent time with the guy discussing why he was being fired—the guy invited Dad to dinner. Years later, my dad's boss confided in him that what he had asked him to do was wrong and he admired how my father had handled it. Doing the right thing is not only important to those directly affected, but it is a measure of your character and reputation, something that will follow you for a long time.

Always tell the truth.

Documentaries about successful law enforcement detectives have led me to a thing I believe to be true. Most people, when asking questions, either know the answer or will arrive at the correct answer. One of the biggest mistakes I see people make is making something up in a meeting to impress a boss. The nice thing about telling the truth is you don't have to remember what you made up. In some organizations, the expectation is that everyone in the management chain needs to understand all the details. This is a really unfortunate stance. People can see right through it, and they also know the leadership of a large organization cannot know everything. It's okay to say you don't know and ask for an answer. When a vice president doesn't know something, unless there are extenuating circumstances, they have time to reach out to the people who understand the problem to get the right answer. By giving a wrong answer and then correcting later, you sabotage your credibility.

Admit your mistakes and own them.

We all make mistakes. By taking ownership and acting quickly, you mitigate the negative effects of the mistake and demonstrate your character and your ability to think on your feet. You will also minimize the mistake by correcting it in a positive fashion. I'm a Seattle Seahawks fan. In Superbowl XLIX, the Seahawks made a miraculous comeback and were on the goal line with just a few seconds remaining. Everyone expected the Seahawks to punch in a quick touchdown and win the game. The ball was snaped and Russell Wilson threw an interception on the goal line, effectively ending the game and preventing a Seahawks victory. After the game, both Pete Carroll and Russell Wilson took the blame for the play call and execution. That shows character. (What they should have done is given the ball to Marshawn Lynch to run it in, but they didn't ask me.)

EXERCISES

1. Have you made a big mistake? What did you do about it?

    _____

    _____

    _____

2. Have been asked a tough question that was hard to answer truthfully? What did you say?

    _____

    _____

    _____

CHAPTER 5

TEXTING MY LIFE AWAY

"This life is what you make it. No matter what, you're going to
mess up sometimes, it's a universal truth. But the good part is
you get to decide how you're going to mess it up."

— Marilyn Monroe

THE TECHNOLOGY REVOLUTION

When I grew up, interacting with my friends was simple. We had a rotary dial phone that was physically connected to the wall with a wire. We picked up the phone, dialed a number, and if whoever we were calling wasn't home, we talked to them later. We might get lucky and run into them at our local hot spot, and we always saw them at school. I remember all the troubles we had when the cordless phone was introduced with losing it in the house, but it was progress.

As time went on, cellular phones arrived. These devices showed up in large cases, were very expensive to buy and use, and had limited coverage areas. Typically, these phones were limited to the upper echelon, those who could afford this luxury.

At the same time, pagers were becoming available, but they were used primarily for business purposes. I was assigned one at work, and it was great until I had to call back from a phone connected to the wall.

As technology progressed, the phones got smaller and smaller and became affordable to the point where the average person could buy one. I remember my first cellular phone. It came with a *service plan* with limited minutes, limited number of text messages, and questionable call quality dependent on where you were. With early cell phones, you were very careful about who you called and how long you talked to them.

Next came the BlackBerry. This device was targeted at business executives and enabled email and limited web surfing, typically for company use.

Fast forward to today, and we now have computing devices in our pockets that are more powerful than the computing platforms used to send the Apollo astronauts to the moon.

We talked earlier about how in just over the last 100 years, we took flight and reached the moon. This last 100 years has also seen unprecedented technology changes. True visionaries have led this transformation and the core business structure that enabled it. People working in large companies invented revolutionary devices from the microprocessor, software, and applications that drove continuous new features. These people left the large bureaucratic companies where the ideas began and formed "start-ups" that matured the technology much faster with the help of non-traditional funding known as venture capital. Early on, these visionaries predicted a computer in every house (Bill Gates) and the doubling of transistors in microchips every two years (Gordon Moore). Storage devices have increased capacity dramatically, as well, with memory cards expanding from 40 megabytes (40 million bytes) in 1995 to 128 gigabytes (128,000 million bytes) today. New terms like terabytes (1,000 gigabytes) and zettabyte (1 billion terabytes) are now used, along with petabyte and exabyte to describe information capacity. It all becomes overwhelming, but it highlights how far technology has really come, with many of the advances coming in the last few decades.

With these new devices, the information age arrived, and the software platforms became small communication and computing devices we all carry today. With this, new ways of leveraging and presenting data to the end user introduced a completely new way of doing business, banking, shopping, dating, and interacting with others.

Apple Computer had a successful ad campaign that proclaimed, "There's an app for that," highlighting that many different applications were designed to do almost everything you could imagine. Those apps that didn't exist yet would be created in time by a new breed of people raised in the digital age. A small search engine company that started up as the century changed now, along with the other major online storage companies, has around 1.2 million terabytes of information stored. They have large server farms in remote areas to process and use this data. All of this information and application development transformed these devices from simple communication devices to social platforms. They became the source of interaction between people and moved the information age into the "influence" age. The Millennials generation has really embraced and defined this transformation.

DEMOGRAPHIC CHANGES

Demographical changes are seen every generation, reflecting new economic and societal norms. The "Silent Generation" (born 1925 to 1945) were raised during the Great Depression and World War II. The "Baby Boomers" (born 1946 to 1964) resulted from the population expansion at the end of World War II and the optimism prevalent during the time. "Generation X" (born 1964 to 1980) is, in my opinion, the forgotten generation. Not much is said about this generation because you typically hear about the Baby Boomers and the Millennials. The Millennials (1981 to 1996) and Generation Z (1997 to 2015) are the most recent generations that have grown up with technology as part of their daily lives. Societal and political conflicts often exist between generations. Many have studied generational differences. I am not an expert on this subject and won't venture into this space. But I will share my observations about the different generations in the workplace during my career and the changes I've noticed.

When I was hired at Boeing Company, the Silent Generation was in charge. There was an air of conservatism and detailed thought. It was a time when technology was largely invented by large corporations (not the consumer market) and designs reflected a conservatism based on being able to touch and see the end product. Shortly after I joined Boeing, I was asked to troubleshoot the engine ignition system on the 747-400. Logic is defined by inputs and commands provided by the pilots from the flight deck (turning ignition on/off, engine start, etc.) and general operating status of the airplane and engines. Looking at the drawings for the first time, I saw many relays that opened and closed to allow current to flow between them to control engine ignition and start systems. (A relay is a simple device with a set of electrical contacts that switch when voltage is applied to a coil.) These relays are useful in controlling high current loads with a lower current source. Relays could also be used to develop complex logic for inputs and outputs. I was about to discover this as I started to decipher the design to determine the issue. It took a while, but I figured it out and resolved the problem.

The people who designed this system grew up in a different time and learned different engineering principles. Many did not have extensive experience with computing platforms, and those who did were exposed to the early platforms that typically took up a whole room. They designed the airplane with what they knew and what was required for the design.

After I completed the design, I had a logic diagram of how the system worked and understood how you could accomplish the logic using relays. I went to school probably fifteen to thirty years after most of these folks. Technology by then had evolved to where integrated circuits were more prominent and computing platforms were in their infancy. Looking at the problem, it became clear we could do the same thing with a small integrated circuit board with logic gates installed instead of relays. When I approached my lead engineer with the idea, he said it would not be certifiable. His worldview did not fully embrace how technology had advanced. That function is now a software routine—well beyond my idea.

Soon the Silent Generation retired and left my generation, the Baby Boomers, in charge. We advanced airplane technology, introduced new features with modern approaches, and started a transition from inventing technology to adapting consumer technology. During this time, the consumer market, fueled by personal computing, highlighted how we could leverage the advances and customize and harden them for use in aviation. This was true outside of aviation as well. Automotive, telecommunications, and industrial systems did the same thing. We soon had new designs and changed what was "certifiable." And our advances were centered on our backgrounds and current technology. Gen Xers started pushing these boundaries, but the changes were metered to fit into the Baby Boomers' worldview. The technological advances were just starting, and it wasn't until the cellular phone and related advances hit the consumer markets that we really started seeing significant changes in how to look at designs.

Enter the Millennials. As time went on, the Millennials entered the workforce. These people grew up communicating with a cellular phone and were technically connected to advances in the consumer market. They were deeply embedded in social media platforms and interacted differently. In job interviews with new college graduates, we asked about diversity and situations they might have encountered. One guy's answer described how to effectively communicate with the older generation—not really the answer we were expecting, but relevant. Their school curriculum was different from mine, and it centered on computing platforms with applications and services coming from those applications.

Reward structures are also different for Millennials. They are generally thought to have been raised differently, in an environment where everyone got a trophy and never really failed. In the work environment, you needed to communicate with them differently. There are winners and losers at work, and not everyone gets a trophy. Of course, when I had discussions along these lines with them, they deflected it, saying, "That's not us. That is Generation Z." More detailed information on this subject is readily available. I just know I had to interact differently with Millennials, and after some time, I didn't need to read about the differences. I was living them.

We are now approaching the time when I will be the old timer and resist change. The younger generation looks at problems differently, and they often propose solutions uncomfortable to my generation. I am fortunate to be more closely aligned with these technological advances, and I understand that Millennials will soon be in charge. They will do things differently than the Baby Boomers or Generation X did. This is change, and change is often good, if directed correctly. My generation's task is to clearly define what we did and why we did it to our replacements. From there, I have full faith they will be successful based on our input and their unique background. A generation from now, they will be turning over the reins, and the cycle will repeat.

When I was in a master's program early in my career, my mentor told me you spend ten years learning technical skills. After that, you don't really learn anything new, but you can solve new problems with what you do know. You then spend ten years developing your people skills. After that, you are complete and can solve problems and leverage others to help in doing so. Later, it dawned on me that my ten years of knowledge and technical skills are much different from those of new graduates. While I can still resolve complex problems, the next generation has developed different skills based on current technologies. They are likely better at solving today's problems and more efficient at using today's relevant tools. Since Millennials are becoming the majority in the workforce, I really see the wisdom in the discussion to allow them to change how we do things.

SOCIAL MEDIA IS FOREVER

I don't think the people who developed "social media" truly realized how much it would change our world. The seemingly simple concept of linking people together and allowing them to share thoughts, pictures, and media would, on the surface, appear to be a great way to help connect people. When people post pictures and thoughts, I don't think many understand that those posts will live forever—somewhere, even if you delete them. Some companies will examine your social media accounts to inspect your posts, and some people have lost opportunities because of inappropriate posts. People have been fired after allegations of misconduct were proven based on the individual's own posts. The White House CIO gave a presentation in which she discussed how posts can be a security risk. She told a story of a serviceman who posted a picture while deployed. Trying to mask his location and identity, he cropped out his face, but he forgot about his name on his uniform. In the picture, landmarks were recognizable, and the GPS tagging was turned on, revealing his location and pattern of travel. By monitoring his posts, an adversary could easily see where he was and predict where he would be in the future.

Like most parents in my community, Bonnie and I gave our children cell phones when they were in middle school. They quickly established social media accounts and were texting and posting early on. In 2008, we took a trip to Canada to go skiing at Whistler. We all ski, and my daughters were really excited to visit this world-class resort. We drove up from Seattle, and in crossing the border into Canada, I told them to turn off their phones. At the time, the roaming in Canada was very expensive. Their reaction was priceless. They questioned why we were going and almost wanted to turn back so they could stay connected. Fortunately, this rebellion was short-lived, and skiing became more important than texting. We also travel to Northern Idaho to a camp with no cellular service. At first, the kids were not happy about the prospect of losing service, but after a few hours, they forgot about their phones and really engaged with camping, rafting, and being outdoors—kind of like when I was young. We did drive to where we had service every other day, though, so we could all connect. (I guess I'm addicted as well.)

Jessica learned the hard way that social media can have a boomerang effect. Kids are smart, so after establishing their social media accounts, they made sure my wife and I were not "friends" with access to some posts. That was their way of not sharing some of the things they were up to that they knew they shouldn't be doing. We didn't worry about our parents finding out things as much when I was young. We just made sure no one who might tell your mother was around.

Every year, Bonnie and I visit Las Vegas and attend the Consumer Electronics Show—probably the largest convention on earth. We travel with friends and leave the kids at home with the older, next-door neighbor to watch them. One night while sitting around the pool, my friend showed me a post of my daughter in our hot tub with all her friends—something I had made clear was not allowed. I called her and asked what she was doing. "Just hanging out," she said. "Just hanging out? With Rachel, Mary, and Lisa—in the hot tub?" I replied.

She was silent. I told her I had seen her post and to let me talk to the babysitter (to send everyone home). She couldn't figure out how I had seen the picture, which I used to my advantage until she did figure it out. While my daughter wasn't my friend, her friends are friends of mine and paid informers (what I told her when we talked about it). We had a pretty long discussion on how what is posted can be shared over and over with some going "viral." Inappropriate posts may surface years later. In my day, people only had to worry about physical evidence of past indiscretions, the photo from high school or college, and more than likely, there was only one in existence, if at all. Now, any indiscretion posted can resurface anytime from any number of sources.

As I started to discuss the longevity and possible harm of posts with my daughter and saw a couple of new recruits to our company get job offers pulled, I decided to audit what I had posted. It only takes a moment to post something on Facebook or select any number of pictures and upload them. Facebook does the rest. They put them in a time sequence (for your benefit) and make them easy to examine. Looking at mine, I noticed that in almost every picture I posted, I had a beer in my hand. Looking at them, you might get the idea that I drink a lot and always have a beer in my hand—not a message I really wanted to communicate. I decided to remove those pictures. Removing pictures from Facebook is not easy. You have to do it one at a time and click a couple of times to confirm you want to delete. I could have disabled my account, but if I reenabled it, the pictures would still be there. It took quite a while to delete them, and after that, I was very careful about what I posted, often not even including a picture of myself.

The other thing most people do not really think about is how social media affects your brain. Studies have shown that posting can have several negative effects. Research is showing a marked increase in depression and suicide in teenagers, and anxiety when posting while waiting for positive responses from your friends. Social media is linked to dopamine, a chemical produced in the brain. Dopamine is a key part of feeling pleasure, and it is released when the brain is expecting some form of reward.

Certain pleasurable activities cause this chemical to be released—among them shopping (if you like shopping), having sex, watching or playing sports, drinking alcohol, using drugs, and social media participation. The more you engage in these activities, the more dopamine is released. Someone once said giving a smart phone to a thirteen-year-old is the same as giving them a bottle of alcohol.

Where does this leave us? Social media isn't going away, and it has been commercialized enough that I don't think the social media platforms really have control anymore. The documentary *The Social Dilemma* is based on the premise that social media is all about money and keeping people looking at the screen. If you like nature, the platforms have artificial intelligence engines that know this from your posts and will suggest nature-based themes. If you have political leanings, they offer posts aligned with what they feel your bias is, whether they get it right or not.

The other scary part of social media is all the platforms are connected through your phone and other connected devices. I have an underwater camera I wanted to sell, so I stopped by a local camera shop to ask about it. They couldn't help, so I went into the parking lot to call a friend who scuba dives. He gave me some good ideas, and we hung up. About fifteen minutes later, he called and said he had just received an ad from the camera shop I was parked in front of. All I can think is because the call was initiated from the parking lot, my phone's GPS identified where I was. Based on the call, they saw we were friends on Facebook and put the ad in front of him. To be honest, I don't really know how it happened, just that it did.

In *The Social Dilemma*, data shows people are becoming more radical in their beliefs. In the past, there were far right and far left fringes, but most people were centered in the middle. While some had extreme beliefs, the majority engaged in civil discourse, compromised, and came to an acceptable solution. The data now shows the majority in the middle is starting to spread to the far left and right of the political spectrum. If this continues, we could experience social unrest to rival anything we've seen in the past and be stuck wading through extreme views not based on facts. Because this industry is currently unregulated, many have called for some form of regulatory oversight to hold social media companies accountable for their platforms. Many groups are advocating for such regulation, and many of the executives who helped invent this technology are speaking out against what it has evolved into.

Bottom line: We really need to be aware of how these platforms are collecting our information and what they are doing with it. Don't click on the suggested material and think about cutting the cord all together. I know many who have. I've come close, but I haven't done it. However, I don't really post or use many of the platforms anymore.

SUMMARY

Today's advances in technology are unprecedented and increasing exponentially. The late 1960s TV series *Star Trek* gave us a glimpse of technology unheard of at the time, including communicators that fit in your pocket and a ship with amazing technology. Who would have imagined that within fifty years of the show, we would have portable computing devices that went beyond those communicators and technology that rivaled the engineering design of the *Starship Enterprise*? (Although we still do not have transporters or warp drive.)

These technologies have transformed our world and moved us from an information economy to an influence economy. How we shop, do research, bank, date, find restaurants, figure out how to navigate a large city, and much more is now at our fingertips. We once had to look at a paper map to figure out where to go or figure out the grid system in an address to get to where we were going. We now ask Google Maps for the most direct route, considering traffic. We have apps that will tell us where the cheapest gas is by mining the credit card charges at the establishment from the customers charging their purchases. Yes, almost everything about us is online, and much of it we put online ourselves. I saw a great YouTube video called, "Amazing mind reader reveals his 'gift,'" where "an extremely gifted clairvoyant" stops people on the street to reveal their financial information and other personal facts. At the end, he drops the curtain to show the information is coming from the internet. As the video says—all this information is online, and it may be used against you.

EXERCISES

1. Look up on YouTube and watch Simon Sinek's video on "Millennials in the Workplace" and "Amazing mind reader reveals his 'gift." Any thoughts?

    _____

    _____

    _____

    _____

2. Look through your social media posts. Do they accurately reflect you, and is the message in the posts truly what you want others to believe?

    _____

    _____

    _____

3. Are there any positive aspects of social media?

    _____

    _____

    _____

4. What embarrassing photos, quotes, or views that may seem extreme to others (political, religious, etc.) have you posted? Is this something that really reflects your core beliefs?

    _____

    _____

    _____

CHAPTER 6

WATCHING DR. PHIL

"You can make more friends in two months by becoming
interested in other people than you can in two years by
trying to get other people interested in you."

— Dale Carnegie, *How to Win Friends and Influence People*

TIME FOR DINNER

I had just come home from work on a sunny summer day. I took my
shoes off, sat down in my La-Z-Boy recliner, and turned on the TV. It was
my way of decompressing from work and getting ready to play with the
kids. They were around five and six at the time and full of energy. While
sitting there, my wife Bonnie yelled down to me to pick up the phone—it
was her mother Kathy. I didn't really talk to Kathy on the phone regularly, so a call from her usually meant she had a question or needed help. I
picked up the phone and said hello.

"Turn the TV to Channel 5. You need to see this." I changed the channel.
It was Dr. Phil talking to a couple about something. Kathy said, "You do
this to your kids."

I do, huh? I hung up the phone and started watching. Dr. Phil was trying to help a couple who weren't getting any response from their kids and were constantly yelling at them. (Hum…sounds familiar). I continued to watch. The father said, "I'll yell at the kids to come up to dinner, and they don't come." Phil replied, "What do you do next?"

"I yell at them again."

"Well, if it didn't work the first time, what makes you think it will work the second? You need to make this personal, and yelling is not personal. You need to go into the room, touch them on the shoulders, and say it's time for dinner. You need to show them it's important to you, and they will treat it as important," Dr. Phil said.

I watched a while longer, but I got the message. Shortly after Dr. Phil was done with this couple, my mother-in-law called back.

"You are always yelling at the kids, exactly what the father was complaining about. You need to do something about it," Kathy said.

We talked a little more, and I could tell she wanted to continue, but I made up an excuse and ended the call. Message received.

I turned the TV back to my show and resumed lounging. After about thirty minutes, Bonnie yelled to me to come upstairs for dinner. I thought, *Why is it okay for her to yell at me, but not for me to yell to the kids?* Out of self-preservation, I let that fleeting thought go. I went upstairs and helped set the table and get things ready to eat.

Meanwhile, the kids went downstairs and took over the TV. When it was time for dinner, Bonnie asked me to go get the kids. What did I do? I yelled for them to come upstairs and got no response.

My brief moment with Dr. Phil came back into focus. I could picture myself on stage with him while he repeated exactly what he had told the other father. I decided to take Dr. Phil's advice and try this new personal touch. I didn't yell again, which would have been my normal next move. I went downstairs, turned off the TV, and calmly said to the kids, "It's time for dinner." They both looked at me, got up, and went upstairs to the dinner table. I was shocked.

Bonnie was surprised as well. She knew the drill and got the food on the table accordingly, so this new way put her behind schedule. The kids were at the table, and I was right behind them. This stuff really worked.

I had to do it again the next night, but after that, when I called them up (instead of yelling), they would generally come up. If they didn't, they knew I'd be down shortly with a personal invitation. They say it takes about three days to change behaviors in children; in this case, that estimate was spot on. Funny thing was it was actually easier and less of a headache than continually yelling. I started doing this for everything I asked the kids to do. If you show them it's important to you, they will prioritize it.

Of course, children being children, and often having myself referred to as a child, it became a game at times. On one occasion, I asked the kids to go to bed. My oldest daughter, Jessica, turned to me and said, "No, and you can't make me!" Such defiance from a six-year-old. I calmly went over to her and said, "I hate to tell you this, but unfortunately, you were born a girl, and for the rest of your life, I'll probably be bigger than you. If you were a boy, sooner or later you'd get stronger than me, but you were born a girl." I then put her into a fireman's carry and took her up to her bedroom. I set her down (gently), said goodnight, and closed the door. For the next several weeks, my kids would randomly refuse to go to bed, and it became standard practice that I would give each a fireman's carry to their rooms.

MY SECOND FAMILY

I became a manager about ten years into my career. I was pretty excited—it was a big promotion, and I would be responsible for up to thirty people installing in-flight entertainment on airplanes. Prior to this, I was a lead engineer with around five or six employees and had filled in when my manager was on vacation or out of the office. When I got the promotion, it didn't take long for me to understand that filling in for my manager was nothing like actually being the manager. As an engineer, I had a feel for which other engineers respected me, liked me, or could not care less about me. When I became a manager, that all changed. Suddenly, those I was confident didn't like or respect me came in to tell me what a great engineer I was and how they really respected me. They would then give me a little test to gauge how easy of a manager I'd be. These tests would be in the form of lobbying to replace me as lead or assigning significant new projects to them. Some came in to say they didn't make enough money and asked if I could look into it. I became a pretty popular guy.

The next thing that happened was I got the secret file with everyone's personal information, including how much they made. I was surprised by a few, but what really caught me by surprise was how many actually made more than I did as their boss. I also found out that one employee was on corrective action, which I would have to deal with. The reality of the management role was not what I thought it was or what I was told. Talking to an engineer who was interested in management about five years later, I was brutally honest. He decided not to apply.

My group tested me, and I failed a few times, but I figured out the whole gig pretty quickly. You have a small window of opportunity to take advantage of someone new in a position before they get smart or get advice from other managers. I soon figured out that if I didn't know the right answer, I'd either just tell people no or tell them I'd ask my manager. That ended the testing pretty quickly and was advice I would regularly give new managers.

While I was getting used to my new life as an engineering manager, I was also adjusting my life to accommodate being a parent for the first time. What I started to see quickly was similarities between the two situations. We would host birthday parties for our kids and, in short order, discover that by themselves they could be a challenge, but in a group, they could get out of control. Same with my work family. Alone, they were professional, but in a group, they digressed. When laser pointers were first introduced, my engineers got ahold of about ten of them and proceeded to play laser tag in the office. When I discovered it and walked around the cubicles, they would see me coming, quickly put them away, and sit down at their desks, a few even chuckling under their breath that *they got away with it.*

Early in my career, we would play pranks on each other—some by today's standards would mean time off work if caught. One involved a box fan, paper punches, and a remote control. I fell for this one and had paper punches sprinkled over my head when I activated the remote and the fan turned on as the group sang "Let It Snow." On another occasion, I caught an engineer lining my desk drawer with plastic. On my desktop was a goldfish. They were going to fill my drawer up with water and release the goldfish. We had someone reverse the keys on the telephone. Instead of 123 456 789, they went 321 654 987. I didn't think too much of this one until we watched the victim try to dial a number. Another time one employee Saran-Wrapped another's car in the parking garage. The target actually turned it around on the employee by getting others in the group to testify that he hadn't come into work that day (they hit the wrong car); then, with the help of a Boeing security guard, he started "investigating" vandalism in the parking lot.

As the manager, I was the adult in this environment, so when things got heated, I had to deescalate the situation or get help to do so. Mostly, I had to deal with employees arguing with each other, some yelling at the top of their lungs. Sometimes there were fights over who owned a desk— two managers were let go for that one when they traded punches. After watching Dr. Phil the first time, I started tuning in randomly and quickly learned that his lessons were not only for my family, but for my group. I would test them out at home and then deploy them at work.

I also soon discovered that things I would do with my family worked at the office as well. Remember earlier about yelling at kids? I used that at work. As the boss, you often have to assign people to do work that may not be popular. In one case, we had a problem on the flight line that would keep someone at work pretty late. I would often just tell someone to go out and take care of it, but then I decided to try some of Dr. Phil's advice. If you want people to understand things are important to you, you need to show them by asking differently and giving it a personal touch. So I went up to one of the engineers and asked him if he'd go out to the flight line to check up on a problem. This caught him by surprise. I normally didn't ask, and he noticed that and smiled at me. He said, "You're asking me to look into it?" I said, "Yes, and if you can't do it, I can get someone else to look into it, but you're really the best person to help." He said, "I'd be glad to help you out." I was surprised. Not only did he go out to help, knowing he'd be at work pretty late, but I think he genuinely appreciated my acknowledging my trust in him. This was not what had normally happened. After this encounter, it became standard operating practice. No longer would I tell people what to do. I'd ask if they would do it. It was a very subtle change, but very effective.

As I progressed into higher levels of management, I became responsible for managers who were responsible for the engineers. In one situation, a group was not performing to my expectations, so I decided to make a change. This group was full of very experienced engineers who understood the technology and how to put it onto the airplane very well—they were just doing more than required and we were falling behind. When they found out I was going to make a change, they scheduled a meeting with me to explain how great their manager was and try to convince me not to make the change. What was really going on is they were driving the group so the manager in the group could not challenge them. One good thing about growing up in the same group is, over time, you see patterns with people and behaviors, and this was one instance of that. They didn't want to lose their power to drive the group by having me put a stronger manager in place who would hold them accountable. It was an interesting dynamic, and not one I expected initially, but in retrospect, I could see how they were still testing me.

REORGANIZING

One of the most controversial tasks in an organization is figuring out how to formally organize the group. In a large company, this is even more complex. In my Boeing training, we spent a good deal of time discussing this. The ultimate message was no perfect way really exists to organize.

You needed to list the pros and cons of each different model, then pick the one with more positives. Over time, the pros and cons change and will necessitate another change to build from where the group was and maximize the positives.

It's also important to randomly change leaders. While the organizational leader becomes very knowledgeable and has history with a group, they may develop blind spots that will not be exposed without a change. When I retired after thirty-five years, I had been in the same group for close to twenty-five years. With this longevity, I was able to push back on bad ideas from my leadership and provide insight on decisions based on historical perspectives. When I left, my replacement also had this level of understanding, but moving into my role (a promotion) would require him to ask basic questions, and by doing so, he would expose blind spots I had developed. Change is always good if you are thoughtful about it and put the right leadership in place.

You can complete tasks and organize teams in many ways. The Agile methodology of managing projects leverages teams that come together to accomplish a task, then dissolve, as another team is pulled together to accomplish the next task. Along with this flux, you also hear about people who have many bosses, which happens when you are supporting multiple programs. At the end of the day, though, you have one manager responsible for your wellbeing and evaluating your performance, no matter how many bosses you may take direction from.

How this boss operates determines the group culture and how the group completes tasks. When it comes down to it, we only have two major ways to organize at the big picture level—functional or program organizations. The two are very different, and each has its pros and cons. Early on, I was in a functional organization that was morphing into a program organization. It was a very big change for the company at the time.

Simultaneously, the defense side of Boeing was making a similarly huge change, but they were going from a program organization to a functional one. At the Boeing Leadership Center, leaders from all over the company came together to discuss things like this. It was interesting to listen to the other side talk about how bad it was going to be moving to a function-based organization from a program one. The reasons were almost identical to our reasons for concern over the change but going the other way. I realized the problem was probably not how we were organized, but change itself and how it would push us out of our comfort zone.

In a functional organization, all of the engineering staff works in a central organization. Programs define work packages, and the functional organization provides staff to get the project up and working, providing support to the program. In this kind of organization, leveraging common designs across different programs or platforms becomes a strength and gives you the ability to dynamically add staff to programs that may need additional staffing at any point in the process.

The success of individuals in the organization is measured by the functional leadership based on how effective the individual was at supporting all the projects. This leads a work culture to look at all programs equally and work to balance the needs of all.

One drawback of this model is that a functional organization is typically a cost center and must provide work estimates to the programs it will be involved in to gain funding to adequately staff the projects. When times are good, a functional organization can effectively request resources from the profit centers (programs) and staff their projects adequately. When times are lean, this can become a challenging exercise.

Maslow's Hierarchy of Needs defines five levels that drive an individual's behavior, and the same is true in organizations. At the core are the physiological needs—those things needed to survive. The next levels are safety, love, a sense of belonging, esteem, and self-actualization. Many organizations are driven by minimizing costs, which, at times, leads to setting unrealistic goals. That pulls the program into survival mode, and in this mode, the organization will ensure direct program support is provided for before nourishing the functional organization or outside entities. Functional organizational culture is diametrically opposed to program culture. In a program culture, the program is number one; all others come second.

A program organization is just the opposite. The people needed to accomplish the statement of work all report to the program manager. (The statement of work [SOW] is a legally binding document that captures and defines all aspects of the execution of a project scope of work.) The line of sight is direct, with a singular focus on program priorities. Program organizations are very effective at completing tasks, but in the drive to develop systems or work packages, other programs' needs are often neglected.

In addition, the SOW is often fully staffed, sometimes creating duplication of effort with similar design activities. At the program level, this overlap is addressed by factoring in staffing, and since the program manager has a direct line of sight to program leadership, staffing is often fully addressed. In this model, staffing and resource needs are very clear and are factored in. This may include surge capacity, the ability to add resources when the project requires them, but this becomes difficult when requesting help from other programs with their own singular focus and priorities.

At Boeing, we had designs that used common parts on all models of airplanes. One program decided to change their version of the part to optimize it for their purpose. While this worked out for them, we ended up having to maintain two parts, and all the programs had to pay for this. This extra cost and possible source of errors was overlooked when developing the business case because the program leads did not think it affected them—but it did. In this model, on the whole, you generally have more staff to focus on program priorities than you would in a functional model, and often programs were generally willing to pay to color outside the lines.

The differences between functional and program models can be seen in the big picture with thousands of employees involved and also in a workgroup of thirty. When I became a manager, I didn't like how the group was organized, so I decided to change it. The group pushed back and tried to convince me all was well. I proceeded anyway, and we had a discussion in the group meeting. Everyone had an opinion, and the meeting became a little chaotic.

I decided to let anyone who wanted to present their thoughts. I gave them the high-level requirements and some constraints. Then I cut them loose, telling them to schedule a meeting when they had something to present. Any presentation would include the entire group. The next week, we had seven different meetings in which we listened to all the different ideas.

The meetings had the desired effect—the whole group realized that organizing a workgroup wasn't easy—in fact, it was quite difficult to create the perfect organization. I listened and didn't comment on the merits of any of the plans. I just asked questions to clarify some of their thoughts and how they would address different situations. This exercise was unique, and I think it created a bond between myself and the group and between the group members. They were all in it together, and I was listening to them.

The next week, I presented the group organization and the changes "we" were going to make. I tried to address all their presentations, giving my thoughts on each. While the new organization didn't really change from my initial thoughts, they all had input and a vested interest in making it successful. I also vowed that if we made a mistake, I'd admit it, and we'd correct it. One of the biggest mistakes new managers make is not fully implementing a decision. Another is not changing something if it doesn't work after it is implemented. Over the years, I frequently admitted a decision was wrong and took steps to fix it.

Taking this idea to the next level, when I was a senior manager, many in the group were complaining we weren't organized efficiently and the processes for making changes in some of the systems we were working on needed to be updated. I decided to perform a similar exercise to the one above, but this time, I included only the first line managers and not the senior managers they reported to. It was fun—the first line managers really took ownership in an environment where they could speak freely about their managers' performance and how the line managers would organize the workflow without fear of offending their managers.

The senior managers were a little taken aback by the process and uncomfortable with it. Normally, they would work with me on these types of changes and inform their people of the decisions made. Looking at human behavior, for the most part, people will protect their personal environment, and in this case, who worked for them and how. After a few meetings, we all came together to discuss the changes. The meetings with the first line managers gave me insight into how things were working and helped realign the people to respond to the changes in technology and systems we were installing.

SUMMARY

Managing people and raising children are pretty similar. The real lesson is how you communicate and interact with them. The most effective managers I have worked for understood this and didn't tell you what to do but would ask, "What do you think we should do?" Their job is to help you get to the right answer. What most employees don't fully comprehend is their bosses really don't know the answers, and the higher up in the organization they are, the less likely they will know the right answer. Their job is to get you resources, help you, and clear your roadblocks.

How you interact, communicate, and show empathy is key for getting the most out of people, no matter if they are your family at home or at work. Everyone wants to feel valued, and it really doesn't take that much to personally thank people or ask for their opinions.

Last, including everyone in the discussion is imperative. I watched a vice president formulate a plan to address a large issue in a back room with some key people (myself being one) and developing a strategy for implementing it. I thought, *Great, the big boss knows what to do and he'll just tell everyone.* That is not what happened. His plan was good, but watching him work a room of 200 very opinionated, experienced engineers to get their buy-in was remarkable. He asked the room the same questions he had asked us in the back room, but by having the meeting with us beforehand, he understood the issues involved. Then he would propose a solution opposite to what we had discussed and wait for the crowd to point out the flaws. In the end, we were pretty much where we thought we'd be after our backroom discussions, but now everyone involved in the change was invested in it and had had an opportunity to provide feedback. One engineer stood up and commented about how hard the change was going to be for his group. The VP acknowledged his concerns and moved on. Both had done their jobs—the engineer pointing out it would be hard and the VP agreeing with him.

EXERCISES

1. Have you ever embraced self-help or feedback about working with people? Was it work related to work or outside of work that could be translated to work?

    _____

    _____

    _____

    _____

    _____

    _____

2. Have you ever been told to do something you didn't agree with? How would you have responded if you were in charge?

_____

_____

_____

_____

3. Think of two or three ways you could acknowledge someone for doing a good job and make your response look natural.

_____

_____

_____

_____

4. Have you been part of an exercise where a major change was made? What were your thoughts?

_____

_____

_____

_____

CHAPTER 7

BUILDING A PLAN

"By failing to prepare, you are preparing to fail."

— Benjamin Franklin, Founding Father of the United States

BUILDING A PLAN

No task, action, or human interaction happens without a plan. While it may not be obvious as we proceed with our daily rituals or activities, everything we do has some form of primitive plan behind it. Going to work has a plan—what time do we wake up, what do we have for breakfast, what do we wear, when do we have to leave, do we need to stop to get gas, and so on. While this seems pretty basic, this simple set of tasks has been performed hundreds of times by those working a forty-hour week, and a high-level plan has been established to help us succeed in this first activity of the day. If your car breaks down during the ride in, you develop a plan to navigate this anomaly—call a tow truck or a friend, figuring out how to get to work and when you can get there and thinking about what others will have to do to complete the tasks you will miss. This all happens in real time as you think about how to navigate the situation.

I don't think most of us realize how much planning we do in the background like this, depending on the situation and activity. Part of this is just "life," and we gain experience over time on how to manage these situations based on our history, feedback from others, or just common sense. New tasks will often make us think about what we need to be prepared for, but we often fall short when things deviate from our expectations.

My nephew Kyle decided one day he would go deer hunting. He had never hunted before, and from what I understood, may not have even fired a rifle. His plan was to go with others who had hunted, and they would help him on his adventure. The first thing was to get properly outfitted—boots, outdoor gear, and an appropriate rifle. Kyle borrowed his mother's rifle, and before this trip, he had never shot it. Second was to ensure he understood the rules and got the needed licenses, etc. The key was understanding what was legal to shoot and what wasn't. Then Kyle needed an emergency plan in case something went wrong. Last, but not least, Kyle needed to know what to do if he actually shot a deer.

While Kyle thought about these, he probably didn't put enough detail into his planning. He had just gotten his license a few weeks earlier. One night, Kyle and his friends decided to go hunting the next day. They were off, driving all night to the location where they would start their adventure. They arrived in eastern Washington around 4:30 a.m. and stopped by a gas station to get some food and buy their deer tags.

They were in good spirits about the experience to come but a little sleep-deprived. As they started, they split into groups to cover more ground. Kyle was paired with an experienced hunter. Somehow Kyle and the experienced hunter got separated. Of course, that was when Kyle sighted a good-sized buck as he got to the top of a large hill. Quickly looking for his partner and not seeing him, Kyle decided to shoot the buck before it got out of range. He took aim, fired, and hit the deer. Regardless of what you may have seen on TV, deer don't necessarily drop where they are when you shoot them. They often run away, and you have to follow them as they bleed out.

Off Kyle went to claim his deer—the only problem was his partner was still nowhere to be found. As Kyle got to the deer, he called his partner, who arrived shortly after. Good, his experienced hunting friend was there—the only problem was that after twenty years of hunting, he had never gotten a deer. Kyle got one on his first day. Now what? Kyle pulled out his cell phone; to his surprise, he had service. Going to YouTube, he searched for "field dressing a deer," found a video detailing the steps, and proceeded to field dress the animal with his friend. Not knowing really anything about field dressing a deer, they patiently followed the instructions and were able to complete the task. Now they had to haul the animal out (about a mile).

At the time, Kyle lived in a high-rise in Seattle and hadn't thought about what to do with the animal when he brought it home. Leave it in his car? Put it in his locker in the parking garage of his apartment? Probably not (although it would have been interesting to bring a deer into the core of Seattle and see the reactions of the other tenants.) Get it processed? Not right away—that needed to be scheduled. In the end, he left it in his friend's garage until it could be processed.

When Kyle told me the story, I was impressed by his ability to accomplish this task, even though his original plan had gone wrong and wasn't really thought out very well. However, he had thought through it in enough detail to leverage his experience outside of the hunting plan to keep the end goal in view.

THE IGNORANT EIGHT

In college, you are exposed to a whole new world—one in which basic plans for accomplishing tasks are no longer sacrosanct and can be deviated from. Add alcohol to the mix and you get lots of really bad plans with potentially really bad outcomes.

Living in a fraternity was probably one of the best experiences of my life. You are suddenly given a level of freedom and many new friends to explore that freedom with. In our fraternity, we had regular parties, probably two per week. Part of our fraternity life was a book we kept in the fraternity house's front lobby. It was a journal anyone could write in at any time. I don't know how long the fraternity had kept these journals, but they went back decades to when my father and grandfather were in the house. At our 100-year anniversary celebration, some of these journals were put on display. The current house members could not relate to the stories in them of what had gone on in college before their time. One current house member commented, "Your average Tuesday night would now get us thrown off of campus for five years." This is likely true—universities have cracked down on some fraternity antics since I left school in the 1980s.

I remember one spring weekend evening when we hosted a semi-private party in our basement bar. Semi-private meant folks could show up who were not specifically invited, and if we liked them, they could stay. This included members from other fraternities, independents, and football or basketball team members. The only difference that evening was some Sig Ep fraternity members showed up. We didn't really like them; they were generally our rivals in the Greek system. To make a long story short, we asked them to leave, they didn't cooperate, and things got a little physical so we ejected them. A few of my brothers took the intrusion personally and started thinking about ways to get back at them. (Nothing really happened short of a couple of egos getting bruised.) These kinds of revenge-plotting exercises were always fun because we'd think of outlandish things to do while continuing to drink and then wake up the next morning laughing about it.

One thing about being with forty-plus ranch and farm boys is they are actually capable of doing a lot of things. The saying goes: Give a farmer or rancher some bailing wire and duct tape and they can fix anything. This isn't that much of an exaggeration. On the range, you are often challenged to fix things or build things with minimal resources.

As it turned out, one of my brothers was helping a family member build a building and had a mixer, sand, and concrete in the barn. While we were thinking about what to do with a rival fraternity, Sigma Epsilon, this store of building materials came to our attention. Eight of my brothers formulated a brilliant plan—brick in the front door of the Sig Ep house. With very little forethought, they (later referred to as the "Ignorant Eight") jumped into a pickup truck in search of bricks. Their total plan to that point was—brick in the Sig Ep front door. Step one, get some bricks. So, off they went in search of bricks…that's as far as they got.

About an hour after the eight went in search of bricks, we got a call from one of the campus residence halls. It was around 2:00 a.m. when a phone call came in. "I need to be picked up, urgently; come and get me!" At the time, almost everyone had a CB radio in their car. We used the CB to dispatch a car to pick up the brother from the residence hall. Talking to him, we found out things had gone wrong and everyone took off in different directions. Within minutes, another call came in. "Come pick me up." We had two cars in the field and got another call. This continued for about an hour before we had picked up five of the eight, except for the brother driving the pickup and a couple of others the eight had planned to haul the bricks in.

The next morning, we still had three missing. Finally, we discovered where they were—the Gallatin County Detention Center. Turns out that in all the planning, no one really thought about where to take the bricks from. Maybe without even knowing it, they had chosen to steal bricks from the Farm Bureau construction site next to the detention center. Somehow, our intrepid brothers didn't even notice the someone watching them load the bricks from his office window who called the sheriff. Had they just taken the bricks and left, they probably would have gotten away, but as one brother told me later, they started having sword fights with rebar at the construction site. When the deputies came , the ignorant eight, minus three, scattered. Those three had no chance to run.

When the Sheriff's Department called, the other five decided to turn themselves in and went to the sheriff's office to join their lost brothers. They were all charged and sent off to face the music. In court, the judge was not happy about their stupidity over stealing bricks from that night next to the detention center. When she asked what they were planning to do with the bricks, one of the eight said, "We were planning to brick up the front door of the Sig Ep house." She did a double-take, then said, "What?" The brother repeated what he'd said, after which I could see the judge smile a little. The ignorant eight were given community service. One brother volunteered for cemetery duty and spent a day digging a grave.

This event is an example of a bad plan, poorly conceived and inadequately planned—or dumb as dirt and not thought out at all. I mean, how would they have gotten the bricks and mortar to the front door? Where would they get power for the mixer, and last, what made them think the Sig Eps would not hear us during the process? Today, when I hear new college graduates brag about their community service, I reply, "When I went to school, community service was court-mandated." I have many other bad plans we explored in college; this one was just the worst.

THE CRAIG LAND COMPANY

Around 2002, my brothers, James and Jason, and I decided to invest in some property in the mountains or on a lake east of Seattle. We set our budget and started looking in the Lake Chelan and Lake Wenatchee areas, only to learn most of the property was out of our price range. I had a friend who had property near Cle Elum Lake, so James and I started looking over there. To our surprise, we found eight, reasonably-priced twenty-acre lots for sale right above my friend's property. We contacted the land company selling them, and over a coffee outside Seattle, we purchased one. We did this without a realtor—something my realtor neighbor was upset about. Most people don't realize you don't need a realtor to manage the sale of property.

We got our property with minimal services. The original intent was to buy and hold the property as an investment, but that quickly changed. The lot was a rectangle situated on a hill with the long portion following the hill's slope. The property had some character, with a relatively flat portion on top that had an excellent view, a middle portion that was somewhat steep with flat areas, and a steep bottom portion with excellent views of the lake—probably the best on the lot. The developer intended for us to build on the top, so that is where he put the power vault. After surveying the lot, we decided we wanted to build in the middle of the lot, off a logging road that went up into the forest. We had to bring power in. The road was used by my friend to get snowmobiles and ATVs into the forest. We also discovered that first winter that it was where the snowmobile groomer started his run.

The first year we essentially camped on the lot and explored the area. The development below was very large with an extensive road system. One day, a road grader was onsite smoothing it out and repairing the winter damage. I have said again and again, and cannot emphasize it enough, that getting along with people is critical. Our neighbor up there (see Chapter 2) was creating problems with the people below us, and I became their outlet and mediator, helping everyone to get along. I approached the heavy machine operator and asked if he had time to do some work on our property. He knew who I was and said he'd come up later when he was finished below. When he finally came up, he dropped his blade, smoothed out our access road, and came up to where we were camping.

Now, this property was still raw, but there was an old logging road where we were camping, and it continued on through our property. I asked if he could smooth it out and widen it a little in a couple of areas. It is amazing what you can do with a road grader and an experienced operator. He dropped his blade and proceeded to drive up the old road, taking out brush and clearing the road. He then made a couple of more passes, made large clearings for us in a couple of places, and pushed down some smaller trees. The whole thing took maybe fifteen minutes. I gave him $200 cash and thanked him. He was surprised by my gift, thanked me, and left.

With the area cleared, we found our building site was much better than the top of the lot. The developer agreed once he came up to see how we were doing. Step one of many was complete—we had a build site.

Lesson 1 – Understand the Rules

Something going on in parallel was a change to the twenty-acre lot size. The developer petitioned the county to allow three-acre lots and they approved. With this new rule in place, we decided to do a short plat to divide our twenty acres into four lots—three three-acre lots and a ten-plus acre lot where our house would go. We discussed this with the developer and survey company, and they concurred with our plan. We had the drawings put together in the package required by the county to revise the lot. At the same time, we were working on the building plans and building permits to start construction. This became Lesson 1. Before we moved forward with either, we should have paused and reviewed what we were doing. We did not and ended up being committed to both without realizing how the timing of each could create issues.

The twenty-acre lots were good to build on, assuming you had water, power, and septic—all feasible. The lots were on a hill, and to get to them, you had to drive up a steep, narrow road for about two miles. At the time of the original plat for the twenty acres, the road met county standards. Over time, though, the county standards changed and required a wider road, had slope requirements, and required improvements that didn't exist on the current road. Being on a mountain to bring the road up to county standards would be a challenge. With the short plat we were planning, we would have to bring the road up to current standards to build on the lots.

We filed the short plat, and a week or two later, filed for the building permit. This simple timing error changed our building permit, so it required us to update the road. Now, this was the original plan; it was not something we had really investigated, and in the end, the other lot owner who was going to share in the building cost backed out, so we never did upgrade the road. At the end of construction, I could not get a certificate of occupancy because of the road issue and had to file for a variance with the county. While it was approved, it was not a simple task. Had we applied for a building permit first, then the short plat, we could have avoided this issue all together. You need to understand not only what you are going to do, but the rules that govern it.

Lesson 2 – Be Careful What You Ask For

Our original plan was to build a simple structure and then follow up with a monster log cabin when we had the funds. We were required to have a place to keep the toys (snowmobiles, ATVs, etc.) and a living space. We decided on a simple, two-story A-frame with a large garage below and living space above. We reviewed the floor plans and got feedback from others. It looked good. We even had a loft on the second floor based on the roof's pitch. We found an architect and started working on the detailed plans. While working with him, we documented some high-level requirements:

- Double door opening to a deck on the front
- Thirty-six by thirty-six-foot structure with open floors
- Covered deck
- Ten-foot-tall garage

old the beam I needed and ordered it. I hitched my single axle trailer to my pickup and headed down to Seaport Steel to pick it up. I arrived to find semis loaded with bridge girders and industrial building steel. I was a little out of place. When I went into the office, the guy sized me up immediately. He knew I really didn't know what I was getting. He got on the radio and had the beam pulled. He pointed into the distance at what looked like a toothpick compared to what they were loading onto the other trucks.

The metal guy said the beam only came in twenty-foot sticks and asked if I wanted it cut. I said "No, we'll deal with it onsite." He laughed, and said, "This is hardened steel. I doubt you have anything that will cut it." (Again, he understood I didn't really know what I was getting.) I picked up on his message and called up to the site, twice, to verify the length needed. (Measure twice, cut once.) I gave the guy the measurement. The steel beam stopped about halfway to my truck, dropped down onto a table, and was cut in a process that looked like a hot knife going through butter, but with sparks.

They loaded the steel onto my trailer, and I was off. As I drove off, I thought, *How do I secure this? It is so heavy I'm not sure just strapping it down will work*, so I pulled over and nailed some boards into the bed of my trailer to keep the beam from moving around.

When I got up to the site, we faced the chore of hoisting a 1,000-pound steel beam off of my trailer and hoisting it sixteen feet into the air. We tried for a while, but we finally decided to call someone I knew nearby to bring a crane to put the beam in place.

When we got the building plans, it called for "engineered" lumber from Boise Cascade. Boise Cascade engineered lumber is pretty standard stuff

- Six-foot walls on the second floor

- Open ceiling in the structure

Once the plans were completed and approved by the count
off to the races. We had the concrete work completed, lumb
delivered, and started to build. This was the really fun part—yc
lumber and start creating something. The garage walls went u
support structure for the second floor was put in place. Part of
open floor was having some large support beams. Getting tho.
was challenging, but with some help from friends and some lil
rowed, we got the first floor completed.

As we started on the second floor, it became apparent the stru
much bigger than we had imagined. With a ten-foot first floc
eight- by twelve-foot pitched roof, the peak was close to thirt
the ground. During this part of construction, I noticed a fe
were missing from our lumber package—particularly, the larg
It turned out they were custom items I needed to special ordei
them was a steel I-beam. I understood the large beam on the rid
structure, but the steel beam was a surprise. When I called the a
he said my requirement of two doors opening onto the deck in
ter of the structure required a steel beam to carry the roof load.
asked what the difference would have been if I had just two doc
a post between them. He said, "Oh, you'd only have needed a s
by six-inch wood post." This was something I should have caugh
reviewing the plans. By not reviewing the detail, I missed this anc
fully understand the design implication of my requirement of two
opening in the center of the structure.

Let me describe how I got the steel I-beam. I found a place in Seatt in building; it's used in posts, beams, and floor joists. Our architect was from Ellensburg, Washington, and all of the construction east of the Cascades was designed to use Boise Cascade lumber. To use engineered lumber, you need an engineered lumber plan from the manufacturer. The architect uses a computer program that Boise Cascade provides, and the specifications are included in the building permit. My building permit had a Boise Cascade engineered floor plan approved. When I went to purchase the lumber, the lumber yard in Seattle replaced it with Weyerhaeuser engineered lumber. Being an engineer, I reviewed the specs for both and found them to be essentially identical, and I agreed to replace the Boise Cascade with Weyerhaeuser floor joists. After we had the floor in, the architect noticed we used a different lumber manufacturer and said the joists were not part of the plan and wouldn't pass inspection. Since I used Weyerhaeuser lumber, I needed an engineered plan from that. This was not something I could undo. The architect did not have software to do the plan, and the lumber company said I should have followed the specifications, even though they had pushed the change on me. This started two weeks of discussions with Weyerhaeuser engineering to get them to provide me with a plan. I had to get the architect involved to describe how the entire structure came together. After two weeks, I had a plan. Had I just understood the implications of "engineered" wood and insisted on the correct manufacturer, all of this would have been avoided. Also, during those two weeks, I had to shut the construction down and one of the framers left for other work.

The six-foot walls were the next mistake we dealt with. With the steep pitch, they really didn't create a space problem, but they made it hard to build and, in a couple of cases, adapt to accommodate a shorter wall. We took eight-foot two-by-fours and cut them down to six feet. Leaving the walls at eight feet would have made the building of the second floor much easier and the finished structure better overall.

The last issue was my request for a stick-framed roof to give us a high ceiling. This required an eight-inch by thirty-six-inch by thirty-foot beam at the ridge and the structure to hold it in place. Because of the span and roof loading, the plans called for two-inch by twelve-inch structural select lumber for the roof joists, doubled up every sixteen inches. On the plan, it looked pretty straightforward, but getting a beam that large thirty feet into the air and then placing 100 or more two-inch by twelve-inch by twenty-four-foot roof joists in place was a significant task. This wood is probably the most expensive we purchased to date, and it took more than a week to put all the joists in place. I found out later if I had agreed to a lesser pitch inside, we could have used scissor trusses instead, avoiding the beam and all of the joists. A truss package would have been cheaper and would have been in place in one day since they delivered the package to the roof.

I did not take the time to understand what I was really building upfront. As we went along, I was forced to understand the building and all the detail that went into the plan. I should have understood what I was building upfront. Everything in the plan was what I had asked for, but I never reviewed with the architect in detail why I needed a steel I-beam or options for roof framing.

Lesson 3 – Be Aware of Scope Creep

We started this project with a plan and options for the building. As we started, we decided we should change some of the plan's basic elements. The first one was the siding. On buildings, the sheeting for the walls is typically OSB or oriented strand board, an engineered wood made by compressing layers of wood strands and adhesives. It is typically less expensive than plywood. While there are pros and cons to each, we decided to use plywood in the entire structure. The cost difference was not large per sheet, but for the entire structure, it probably added several thousand dollars.

We then looked at the siding and decided we did not want ordinary engineered siding as the plans called for. We upgraded to cedar siding, which was expensive. As part of the siding, the deck railing was also a pretty simple structure, and to keep the idea of an outdoor retreat, we revised the deck railing to use logs. To fabricate the railing added cost and time.

We then looked inside and decided to replace all the doors with knotty alder and upgrade the kitchen cabinets to the same material. For the ceiling, we installed one-by-six tongue-and-groove boards instead of sheetrock. It gave it more of a cabin feel.

To top off the scope creep we installed an in-floor heating system instead of a gas stove. My brother James and I talked right before we poured the garage floor and decided we should put in-floor heating tubes in before the pour just in case we wanted to put them in later. A week later, the cabin was equipped with an in-floor heating system that cost nearly $15,000.

James and I caused a lot more scope creep, but the big ones are listed above. While we went into the changes with our eyes wide open, we added significant cost and slowed the build schedule significantly. For every change, we had to stop, revise what we were doing, and in some cases, replace the material. We did say no to a few things, but it was not from a cost perspective, only timing and schedule.

Lesson 4 – Create a Flexible Schedule

The one key thing I would change if I were to do this project again would be to better understand the schedule and timing for things. We went into this project eager to get a structure built, and we were lucky to get the roof installed before the first snow (by a week). With snow loads approaching 300 pounds per square foot, snow on an incomplete structure could cause significant damage.

We started the project in the spring once the snow was mostly gone. We submitted the plans to the county and had approval by the end of June. You could not get concrete trucks or lumber trucks up the road in the winter, so June became our starting point. Starting, we needed to get some heavy equipment in, and because of the slope and position of the structure, we had to dig into the hillside to clear a space. Once that was complete, we had the concrete for the footer forms put in place. This took a couple of days, and we then needed to get it inspected. It took probably a week to get the inspector notified and onsite to sign off the footers. We got the approval the first week of July and poured the foundation the following week. We then had to remove the forms and repeat the process for building the walls. This took a week or two. This left the garage floor, which was completed at the end of July. It was August before we started building the structure in earnest. The opportunities for lessons learned described above caused the project to creep into late September, and it was early October before we were ready to put the roof on.

Probably the biggest mistake we made was in estimating how long things would take and our optimistic view that we would get things done much quicker. I've experienced this in business as well when schedules don't reflect reality. In my case, we got the roof on in time, but it was close.

SUMMARY

I have never experienced or heard of a plan that was actually completed perfectly and on schedule—or even one that followed the planned sequence of events. Planning is really about making us think about actions, identify risks, and mitigate issues as they surface. The more complex the task, the more likely the plan will be complex. People spend their entire careers devising methods for planning and managing projects. In my personal and professional experience, I've learned four primary lessons:

1 – Understand the rules. Everything has constraints either from the product market, regulations, or company policies. Understanding the rules can keep you out of trouble with anything from simple issues to regulatory issues that can involve civil or criminal charges.

2 – Be careful about what you ask for. In my example, I presented myself to the architect as a very knowledgeable builder. He took my direction without question, and when I asked him about it after the fact, he said I seemed to know what I was doing. Understand what you're building upfront. As you build or develop a product, sooner or later all the details will become important, and if you don't understand some of the details, they can create significant rework and added cost.

3 – Beware of scope creep. This happens in every project in response to requests for changes to enhance or improve the product. Be aware and create a process to review these changes and fully understand what they mean to your project from both a cost and schedule perspective. Change is normal, and with complex projects, inevitable. Keep apprised of the changes and manage them.

4 – Create a flexible schedule. Last, understand the overall plan and how long it will take to complete the project. Build a plan with constraints that drive you to move to the next stage and understand the timing and dependencies of all the elements of the project.

EXERCISES

1. Think about ordinary tasks and actions you complete daily and how they get completed. What is the unspoken plan for each task you "just know" how to do?

   _____

   _____

   _____

2. Have you set out to do something without really thinking about it? How did it turn out?

   _____

   _____

   _____

3. For a task you planned, list a few items that helped it go well. List a few items that probably were not reviewed in a timely manner.

   _____

   _____

   _____

4. Have you been involved in a major project? How did it go? Was the plan adequate to complete the task?

_____

_____

_____

CHAPTER 8

GETTING THE FOUNDATION RIGHT

"Insanity is doing the same thing, over and over
again, but expecting different results."

— Author Unknown

POOR DESIGN

Those who work on cars know that some car designs bring thoughts of pain and agony. Some designs require you to lift the engine off its mounts to change an alternator. Some foreign cars' maintenance is very expensive because you almost have to take the car apart to get at some components. Some cars have a "timing belt" that needs to be changed around 75,000 miles. If you forget and the belt breaks, you could be looking at major engine repair.

This is also true in many other areas. Why is a shutoff valve in your house hard to find or get to? Why do stores use fasteners that don't allow you to open something without breaking it? Why do all electronic devices have different charging cords? Why can't Apple and Android phones agree on a common charger? These issues all stem from the creator not thinking about the end result and not getting the foundation right.

The timing belt hits home for me. I forgot to change it on one of my cars, and at 85,000 miles, it broke. It caused some of the engine valves to get damaged and amounted to a significant charge to repair. I was told it could have been worse. I never had a timing belt problem on my 1969 Mustang because it had a chain, not a fabric belt. Using a fabric belt was a decision an automotive engineer made either to reduce cost, create a maintenance job later, or maybe both. Both are poor excuses. Doing things right upfront would have eliminated my issue, so such issues are something we should discuss briefly.

BUILDING THE CABIN

In the last chapter, we discussed the plan and mistakes made during our cabin's planning process and their impact on the overall project. As you build something, how you build it and how you adapt to issues can have a significant impact upon the finished produce, both good or bad. In this project, we had both, but unknowingly, we got lucky when we were re-ferred to a concrete contractor and carpenter to start building the struc-ture. Not knowing really what I was doing, I was flying by the seat of my pants a little. When we originally looked at building, we discovered the project manager had a hefty fee in the bid, something that did not sit well with me—it seemed too much. Now, I know many different folks in the construction trades. A friend who was a concrete contractor essentially laid out what I needed to do:

- Pour the foundation.

- Send the plans to a lumber company to get a lumber package put together.
- Hire a framer to do the framing and rough construction.
- Hire a plumber and electrician to put the plumbing and electrical wiring in.
- Hire a company to install the insulation.
- Hire a company to install Sheetrock.
- Hire a company to do the roofing.

I think you get the drift. The process seemed pretty straightforward and something I could easily do part time (I had a full-time job at the time.)

I agreed, sent the plans to a local lumber company, and asked my friend to bid out the concrete work. I did the same with the rest of the major functions, but not as formally. I just got the rough costs so I would understand what I was committing to. The numbers lined up with my expectations for a better structure than what the developers were proposing at a little lower cost. My brother and I were also going to put in sweat equity, which brought the numbers down.

Time to get started…. My friend scheduled the concrete pour, came up with a crew to make sure the excavation was good, and started setting up forms. He had a laser transit, and at one point, he had his folks remove an entire wall of forms because they were a little out of line. I'm not sure if he would have done this on someone else's job, but I think he was really trying to do a good job for me. He also was key in finding the right people to help me. Being in the trades, he had contacts and influence I didn't have.

We poured the foundation (after our big change adding in floor heating) and were ready to start building walls. For major tasks, I would take time off to go up and watch. For the concrete, they brought up a pumper truck for the slab pour. The pumper truck is just that—a concrete truck pours the concrete into a hopper in the pumper truck and it gets pumped wherever the boom is positioned. This was a very large truck and had a large reach. (I poured a slab in my backyard, and they had a pumper truck with a boom going over my house.) Being a technology guy and wireless guy at Boeing, I was fascinated when he put on a fanny pack with a wireless controller for the truck, boom, and concrete pump; opened it up; and synced to the pumper truck. He was able to maneuver the arm and start pumping wirelessly while walking around the site.

Once the concrete was done, it was time to start pounding nails. The lumber package showed up and we took an inventory. Most of the lumber seemed to be there. In talking to folks, I'd learned the lumber takeoff is never 100 percent accurate and will require purchasing extra material as needed. I was ready to go—I had my tool belt on with all the tools I thought I'd need, and I waited for my carpenter to give some direction on the first steps.

The next part was pure luck, and it was based on a recommendation from my concrete contractor. Blaine, the guy who was going to build with me, was actually a finish carpenter and outdoor hunting guide. The cabin was pretty remote, and he loved it. Over time, he set up a camp with a wall tent and wood floors. He would, at times, go for a walk and come back to the construction site with some branches. He would put a branch into a drill, and with some sandpaper, make arrows by spinning the wood and sanding it with the paper. My kind of guy. The other thing he did not do was drink. I've heard stories about construction crews that leave for lunch and do not come back. I didn't have that issue.

Okay…time to get started. To my surprise, Blaine got out a laser transit and started taking measurements of the concrete work. He checked to ensure it was level and properly squared off. I was surprised he would go to this length. It was not what I was expecting. He then got out a disc grinder and started walking around the stub wall, grinding parts of it on the surface. Then he got the laser transit out and remeasured. I was trying to figure out why he was doing this. He probably spent an hour or two looking at the foundation and making adjustments. When Blaine asked who poured the concrete, I said "Don, my concrete contractor." Blaine knew Don and said he had done a very good job. Then he added, "The walls are very straight and right on from a size perspective. The only issue are spots where the concrete is high, which is normal with large pours like this. Most are less than an eighth of an inch off." I said, "That's not much. Why did you fix it?"

"If you get the foundation right, the rest is easy," Blaine said. "The corners are square and everything from sheetrock, trim, and cabinets go up much cleaner. Also, an eighth of an inch can add up over multiple floors where you have a significant gap or rise later on. These are all issues I have to deal with when I come in to do the trim and finish work later on."

It made sense. That was when I realized I had a finish carpenter doing framing. His framing was all spot on. Later, Blaine took me to another job site and showed me what happens when you don't pay attention to the plans or make sure things are square before you start. I saw a partially built structure with three beams joining at a peak at an angle. None of them really fit well and were attached by hundreds of nails. He said no one would know because the sheetrock would cover it, but over time, it would probably crack or have other issues because of the shoddy construction.

Blaine was a perfectionist. My structure was thirty-six by thirty-six feet square. Once the walls were up, Blaine measured corner to corner to check how straight and square the walls were. We had already measured the foundation, so if they were out, it was a framing issue. He measured several times and was making adjustments when he came up to me and said he was nine-sixteenths of an inch out of square. Remember, he's a finish carpenter—to him that's a lot.

Being a smart aleck, I said, "Can't you do any better than that?" Then I got in my truck and went into town for some lumber. When I returned a couple of hours later, he came up to me and said, "I can't get it any better."

Now, on a thirty-six by thirty-six-foot structure, the corner-to-corner measurement is around fifty-one feet or 612 inches. Nine-sixteenths of 612 is a 0.09 percent error—to me that's really, really good work. My smart aleck comment set him back two hours, and I was paying him by the hour. I told him I was kidding, and it was actually very good. After that, I was careful about making off-hand comments.

THE PERGOLA

I really like to build things. When we purchased our home, Bonnie looked at the backyard and had a master plan. Flower gardens, firepit, deck, etc. This master plan was a significant undertaking and something we thought about and worked on for two decades, taking one bite at a time.

One feature that sold me on the house was an outdoor firepit. I love the outdoors, and nothing is better than sitting around a firepit late at night. Improvements to the firepit area were a big part of the master plan. We wanted a concrete slab under and a cover over the firepit so we could go out when it was raining. (We live in Seattle.) That was the plan.

A few years later, we decided it was time to pour the pad for the firepit. As we were preparing the site for the pour, we remembered the plan for a cover over the firepit. We looked at the site and decided a ten-by-twenty-foot structure would be good, and we made sure we had footers for the posts we'd need. We measured, took pictures, and documented where the structure would sit.

A few years later, we decided it was time to build the covering. I did a detailed design, contacted a lumber mill to get some rough-cut timbers, and put up the structure. The structure went up pretty easily because I took the time to think about how to assemble it before starting. The beams and rafters were heavy, so I got a lift to help and picked up some aids to secure them. We now have a covered firepit that closely resembles the big picture plan Bonnie put in place decades earlier.

GETTNG THE BIG THINGS RIGHT

I was still working full time, and while we were building, I was taking two or three days of vacation at a time. At the end of the summer, my boss said he had noticed my absences and that my performance had slipped a little, but he understood what I was doing. I had a tent trailer onsite and spent my nights there eating Pop-Tarts and fast food. Staying in the woods alone is a unique experience, and at times, I'd hear things that scared me a little—like animals passing nearby. Overall, though, it was probably one of the most rewarding times of my life.

Building this structure exposed me to a completely different industry.

As we built and I became aware of issues with the plans, I would call the architect, get a resolution, and document it in a change log (a Boeing artifact). When I showed it to the county guy, he really liked it, and it gave me credibility with him and some leeway with the inspectors. Doing things that were novel to my world, I would write blog posts and introduce them to my work group, with a work spin on them. Most of the lessons I learned were in project management and developing a detailed understanding of the project.

I was working in a technical center where we looked at new designs and features that airlines wanted to install. This was early, upfront stuff that we evaluated and then followed in development. A few years later, I was transferred to the 777 program as the systems lead. I wasn't really excited about the job, but I needed it to progress to higher positions. I was shepherding the final stages of the 777 build, addressing issues, and working on fleet issues. It wasn't long before I realized a lot of little issues were creating cost overruns and problems at the airlines in-service. These weren't the system level issues I was dealing with in my previous job, but the end result of the decisions and design details that had been incorporated in the final product. This is when I realized problems are typically not big, but little. It could be an electronics component that failed early or an oil leak from seals wearing out in the harsh airline environment. These are not things that ground airplanes or that passengers or flight crews are aware of, but things that the airlines need to address to keep the fleet flying efficiently.

This was the origin of my new work philosophy when working on designs in the early stages of development: "You need to get the big things right so we can discover the little things that are the cause of most problems." This tied in with my building experience—I learned that understanding the detailed design, managing scope creep, assuring you understand your baseline, and getting it right from the start are essential. Taking time upfront to understand the requirements and fully flesh them out really makes the job much easier later—even if you have to take more time to get it right.

NEW PROGRAM DEVELOPMENT

One of the best programs I worked on came early in my career as an engineer. It was a new airplane, and we developed several plans—test plan, certification plan, development plan, detailed specification plan, etc. This was several years before the airplane was scheduled to be delivered, and we were introducing some new technology and new ways of building and testing it.

At one point, my manager announced we had a major problem with our specifications and asked for help from senior leadership. I wasn't happy and told him we were all right. He replied, "We're going to ask for help now and get all of our issues resolved. When the airplane gets close to testing, we will not be declaring an emergency, and nobody will remember that we asked for help early on." He was a wise man. He knew we didn't have all the details for the design and some elements of the plan fleshed out. We took a schedule hit, but no one remembered that, and our system was mature at the start of flight testing. All the plans we published formally clearly communicated what we were doing and made it easy to integrate our system with other systems.

SUMMARY

Getting the foundation right is critical. As you are working on a project, if you can't communicate the plan or don't know the details of the design or activity, you are destined for trouble. One of the hardest things for people and companies to do is take the time upfront to plan, make sure the details are defined, and start with a "good foundation." In my experience, when you start without a complete set of requirements or structured plan to develop them, you end up with suboptimal results as the design evolves. You need to start with a good foundation and immediately address issues as they come up. As I was building my cabin, the architect and engineer were frustrated with me for coming in with all the little issues I found. I was not acting like a normal contractor, and they told me to do what I thought was right and we'd see if the inspector caught it. On my cabin, the inspector did not find any issues because I made sure there weren't any to find.

EXERCISES

1. Have you been pressured to start a project or detailed design before you thought you were ready? What did you do?

   _____

   _____

   _____

   _____

   _____

2. Have you ever had a maintenance problem that seemed to be a by-product of poor design?

_____

_____

_____

3. Have you started a project only to have to go back and make significant changes because you didn't think about it enough upfront?

_____

_____

_____

CHAPTER 9

THE SOFT TOUCH

"With pride, there are many curses. With
humility, there come many blessings."

— Ezra Taft Benson

THE SMARTER PERSON IN THE AUDIENCE

Growing up in a rural setting taught me several things, one being everyone seemed to know everyone—from their habits to their deep secrets. When meeting people, initially, I think everyone is a little reserved. You don't start a discussion on politics or controversial subjects until you understand someone's background and general values. In a rural setting, this step is often skipped because you already know everyone's background. Even as a kid, I knew who the bullies were, who got angry quickly, and who I couldn't really get a rise out of.

I also think everyone has a little to a lot of arrogance built in. This can get in the way of discussions, especially if you don't know who you're talking to. One thing I learned the hard way was there is always someone smarter than you in an audience or at a gathering. In presenting at a conference early in my career, I stated firmly what I thought was a fact, only to be corrected by the smarter person in the audience. It was a little humiliating but an important lesson.

After that, I always kept the idea that there was someone smarter than me in the audience in the back of my mind. While I was the expert in what I was presenting, someone might not agree, so I needed to acknowledge the disagreement during the presentation. In one conference where I was presenting, one of the government intelligence people stood up, said I was wrong, and that he could take over an airplane from the ground. I knew he was wrong, but rather than debate him in a public forum, I said I didn't know of a way to do that and would like to understand how it's possible, so I'd like to meet with him after. It was a pretty neutral answer. I had acknowledged his perspective and that terminated the discussion. After my response, though, an Air Force pilot stood up and took him on, saying he was wrong. I didn't know the first guy, but the pilot did, and it turns out the intelligence guy made such inaccurate statements frequently.

Being true to my word, at the next break, I went up to the intelligence person, introduced myself again, and asked him for more information. He looked at me and said, "Oh, you work for Boeing. You can't do this to Boeing aircraft," and walked away. He had known I worked for Boeing during the presentation, so it was obvious to me he was just looking for some attention. I worked with him several times after that, and he did have interesting perspectives, but from that exchange (and many others I had with government and research people), I knew he didn't really understand how airplanes work.

FIGHT OR FLIGHT

Everyone has a fight or flight reaction during stressful situations. If things get difficult, they will either withdraw or engage more intensely. We have all seen this happen with the people we interact with. One of the characters I talked about earlier had been a Marine recon-sniper during the Vietnam War. He had a fight reaction that was very visible, and one of my greatest challenges was responding to it when it surfaced, which it did regularly. When I was promoted into management, he was in my group. He was large and intimidating, especially when he got vocal about things he didn't agree with. I quickly learned that getting into a heated exchange with him would not work, so I started looking for other ways to divert his "passion."

I was also a little afraid of him, initially. He was older and had more years working in the community. It's interesting that we all have people we somewhat avoid because we perceive they may not like us or do not respect us. In working with this person, I quickly learned that none of that is necessarily true and the people we avoid may have the same thoughts about us. The only way to know is to engage them to sort out their true feelings, and in a professional perspective, work on closing the gap to help understand their situation.

The fight or flight reaction is real, and we all react one way or another. When we determine the person's reaction, we can actually interact with them in a more positive manner. If someone usually withdraws when an issue comes up, as a leader, you know they are under stress and can take steps to help mitigate it. The same is true for the person who pushes back. One big positive about Boeing is its commitment to leadership development. As a manager, I was provided the opportunity to attend several leadership classes. One course discussed this subject in detail.

What does it mean when a person who normally withdraws suddenly starts pushing back? What happens when my recon-sniper gets quiet? This is a sign that the issue has become overwhelming, and they feel pushed into a corner. It is something you need to address right away, or at least, you need to know you've pushed them to their breaking point. Once I became aware of this, I started to understand behaviors in the group much better.

I am generally a flight person. I will withdraw from controversial situations to allow others to settle the matter before engaging, but at times when I would push back, I was surprised by how others responded. Because it wasn't my normal behavior, people understood I was being pushed too far. Understanding when a person will be pushed too far will help you communicate with them better and understand elements of the issue they are communicating. If Bonnie suddenly gets quiet during a heated discussion, I know I'm in trouble. If the discussion stays heated, I know it will all probably be okay. Her normal response is more on the fight end of the spectrum.

THE SOFT TOUCH

My group was a technical center or core engineering group. We held much of the detailed technical knowledge and were responsible for much of the testing and formal qualification of the products that were put on all Boeing airplanes. In this role, we would have many discussions with various groups. Some of these groups had a lot of experience putting the products on the airplane and understood the overall processes, and some were doing it for the first time. Being the core engineering group, everyone actually had to work with us to complete the projects, and because of this, we became very arrogant in our behavior and how we treated other groups. It's one thing to be right, another to convince someone else you're right. The second often becomes the challenge, and we spent a lot of time and energy at times convincing others what the right thing to do was.

We had an "aha" moment during one of these interactions. One of my managers was working with another group, one that didn't really appreciate our role and disagreed with us often. One of the discussions became very heated after several meetings. Since they were in a remote location, this was all done via phone. Both sides hung up and my manager came in to inform me this group didn't really know what was going on, so they would have many problems once they got the product onto the airplane and tried to get it certified. I agreed since I had seen it many times before. Almost immediately, the other manager called me and asked if I could join in on the call. He was frustrated and didn't agree with what we were telling him. I said yes.

The next day, I joined the call with my manager arriving late. They started in on the discussion telling me how my group wasn't working with them and didn't understand what they were trying to do. At this point, my manager came into my office, and I hit the mute button on the phone. We started a side discussion and agreed these guys were messed up. All of a sudden, I hear a "What do you think, John?" I had no idea what they were discussing or that they were discussing it with me…. What to do? I responded with a somewhat sarcastic comment, "Well, Dave (the other manager), we could continue the discussion, but I'd like to call you privately and give you my perspective and make sure I understand what you're saying. We're here to support you and want to make sure you understand our perspective." He agreed and the call ended suddenly. I was a little shocked and didn't know if they were really mad at me or if he was going to call. My manager and I looked at each other and wondered what had just happened.

Dave called me back almost immediately and started to lay out the situation. I acknowledged his comments and then calmly discussed why I "thought" (instead of saying I knew) what I did and why he might want to take a different approach. I said my group was there to support, and ultimately, it was his decision. I told him of other programs that had attempted his approach and how they had ended up, but I reiterated it was his decision. This was a 180-degree reversal of how we normally reacted, and I'm not sure why I went down this path. Normally, I would have insisted they do what we say and press on. My manager was listening in and smiling as if to say, "Are you serious? They don't have a clue what to do, and if it goes south, we'll be holding the bag." I know....

A new phone meeting was set up and we joined. This time, Dave asked us to let him lay out his plan. He was essentially going to proceed how we suggested with a few changes. Some of the outspoken people in his group also agreed. What they did not realize is they were telling us what we had been telling them to do in the previous meetings. The meeting ended, and we couldn't believe how it had gone. It was much easier than arguing. It was then their plan, and they were in-charge. They were no longer being told they didn't know what they were doing and saw my group in a different light.

At our next staff meeting, I announced we were no longer going to insist people do as we say. Our new mission was, "We're here to help." We'll give advice and details on how to proceed, but it was their decision to move forward. It dawned on me that other groups had to work with mine. If they had a choice, many would probably go elsewhere. I knew this because we had groups we had to work with that we really didn't want to work with. I wanted people to seek us out and want to work with us.

It was actually a revolutionary change. That simple perspective shift in how we worked with others made our job much easier, and I noticed other groups started to engage us on projects we probably wouldn't have been asked to work on in the past. Our reputation with the programs and with our bosses changed as well from a group that was difficult to work with to one they could engage and get quick turnaround from.

One of these projects involved creating a system from scratch, and the people running it, in my opinion, didn't really know what they were getting into. The old John would have pushed back and told them why it wouldn't work. This time, I engaged them, and instead of telling them why I didn't think their plan would work, I rephrased, focusing on the steps and challenges they would face with what they were proposing. I enlisted several of our experts in workshops and engaged with their supplier to work through the plan. In the end, it became clear they were going to do this no matter what I thought, but by approaching it the way I did, it built a very positive perspective not only on me but my organization. We were able to help in several places, and they appreciated our support. "We're here to help."

SUMMARY

In college, when I belonged to a fraternity, it was not uncommon for the fraternities to play practical jokes on each other. One night, the men's basketball team came and started loading our living room furniture into their car. We blocked them in so they couldn't leave and watched. One of the brothers even held the door open for them as they took things out of the house. They finished up and realized they were blocked in. We had some choices. We could try to get physical with them—probably not a good idea; these were big men. We could call the police, but probably not good as well. We just watched when one of them asked if we knew who owned one of the cars and if we could get it moved. The door holder calmly said, "Why would I move it when you have all our furniture in your car?" Then he said, "Why don't you put it all back and come into the bar with us for a drink." They thought for a moment. By this time, most of the fraternity brothers were present—about forty of us. The basketball team decided to have a drink, and we actually became really good friends with most of them over time.

By now, you should be seeing the common theme in this book—respect for others, acknowledging their perspective, and engaging from a positive perspective. The basketball team realized they had probably made a mistake, but we didn't really confront them. In the end, it became their decision to put the furniture back instead of forcing some other outcome.

Here are a few thoughts from this chapter:

- No matter how smart you are, someone else is always smarter.
- We all have a "fight or flight" instinct. Understanding which one those close to you gravitate toward naturally is important to understanding their state of mind. Also, if someone who normally has a flight reaction moves to a fight reaction, they probably feel cornered.
- Of the many ways to interact with people, taking a "soft touch" and "helping" approach is much more effective and actually less work.

While you may not get direct credit for things, over time, everyone knows you're the one enabling the positive results.

- If you're going to take furniture from a fraternity, make sure your escape path is clear.

EXERCISES

1. Talk about a time you interacted with someone when you may have taken it too far. Did you recognize a change in their behavior?

_____

_____

_____

2. Have you met someone smarter than you? How did you react? Did it change how you interacted with people?

_____

_____

_____

3. Discuss a time when you told someone what to do and how it might have turned out differently if you had asked instead.

_____

_____

_____

CHAPTER 10

WRITING IT DOWN

"Writing, the art of communicating thoughts to the mind through the eye, is the great invention of the world...enabling us to converse with the dead, the absent, and the unborn, at all distances of time and space."

— Abraham Lincoln

THE POWER OF THE WRITTEN WORD

Many have asked me what prompted me to write a book, a self-help book no less. My family, going back on both sides, documented their stories, some better than others. One story that stood out for me was from my great-great-grandfather Josef Küng (anglicized to King) who came here from Switzerland. His autobiography is well-documented with a lot of energy put into editing and adding pictures, including a family tree. It is a fascinating read, especially for me since it involves my heritage. In it, he tells of leaving Switzerland in 1869, departing from Havre, France, and taking the long voyage to New York City. Josef eventually made it out west and ended up in a mining camp in Diamond City, Montana. He documented how he, along with the German immigrants, were looked down upon, could not visit some of the local establishments, and struggled in the early years because they didn't speak English very well. My grandmother told me she was not allowed to speak German. Her parents told her, "We are Americans, and we speak English." (In St. Gallen, they spoke a Swiss variety of standard German.) What a change from today when multiculturalism dictates accommodating all languages.

In 1878, Josef sent for his family. He recorded how hard it was for them to leave Switzerland, parting from their family and friends while knowing they might never see them again. The King, or Küng, family had been residents of Benken in the Canton of St. Gallen, Switzerland. The state archive records the Küng lineage along with its coat of arms, which was awarded to Bernard Küng von Buchberg for service in the famous battle of Marignane in 1515. Grandpa Josef's writings trace the family back much farther, but I was not able to ascertain specific dates. Nonetheless, moving to the New World was a significant sacrifice.

Joseph's manuscript documents his early life with many interesting stories of frontier life and how they survived, moving from a lard-based diet to getting chickens and trading eggs for sugar and other foods. One story describes getting their first herd of cattle and working to get it into the river to save them from a prairie fire, then losing them while oversleeping. It took about a week for his brother to round them up—all by himself. Life was hard in the West, and I am not sure the current generation, including myself, would survive the way they did.

I tell you this not to spend time educating you about my family, although I'm quite proud of what my family accomplished. Most people are proud of their families. I could go into the other side of the family that came from Czechoslovakia. They had it even harder, living initially in a sod house. The Kings at least had a log house.

I tell you this story to emphasize the power and historical relevance of documenting a story. My true inspiration for writing this book was more selfish. I wanted to document my story for my children, grandchildren, and great-grandchildren to read. We all live in a unique time in history, and the things we take for granted today will more than likely be remarkably interesting to later generations. I have lots of stories, with some embedded within this book, but they are not the only stories. One thing that happened shortly before I retired was people were setting up time to talk to me about their careers and to get other advice. I thought it would be better to document the advice I gave while it is fresh in my mind instead of focusing on my story first. I have plenty of time to work on my autobiography later.

The words of my great-great-grandfather's text are now of historical relevance. He documented a time we only seem to relate to now in movies and fiction, which may not be historically accurate. Recently, I visited the OK Corral in Tombstone, Arizona. They have a display where the gunfight took place and a historically accurate account of the location of each man and the events that followed. They got this information from the court proceedings after the gunfight where Wyatt Earp, his brothers Virgil and Morgan, and Doc Holiday were charged with murder. Many witnesses were interviewed right after the event and newspaper articles were written during the trial. Together, these documents compose a historical record and a pretty accurate one with all the different perspectives and analysis of the court proceedings. FYI...they were all freed after a month-long hearing.

The written word has power from a historical, legal, and entertainment perspective. Creating a contract, compiling a proposal, or just documenting your thoughts requires writing something clearly. The quality of the document can void a contract or cause you to lose work based on inadequately highlighting the value of your concept or inadequately describing it in a proposal. In business, it is very important to properly document your statement of work and your processes. By clearly writing these down, you can establish a repeatable process, one you can incrementally revise.

Being retired, I'm getting back into golf. I learned to golf at an early age and know many of the game's fundamentals. If you watch pros on the PGA tour, you'll notice many take a notepad out after each shot. They also document things at the driving range. Golf legend Ben Hogan, in his book *Ben Hogan's Five Lessons: The Modern Fundamentals of Golf,* even talked about the importance of writing down things you have tried and whether they helped. In the book, he documented what he learned, which I have found very useful, although I still struggle finding the perfect shot. The pros take notes to document different swings, grips, or stances to help identify things that will improve their game.

I find a quote from the character "Chaucer" in the movie *A Knight's Tale* insightful and telling of the power of the written word. The main character, William, is of lowly birth. When the knight William serves dies, William takes his place in a tournament. William decides to continue impersonating the knight and enter tournaments so he and the knight's other two servants can eat. Along the road, the three encounter Geoffrey Chaucer, of *Canterbury Tales* fame. Chaucer can provide Patents of Nobility, proving nobility back four generations, something required to enter tournaments. In the movie, Chaucer has a gambling problem, and when we first meet him, he is walking down the road naked. He joins the trio and becomes William's herald, offering poetic and rousing introductions at tournaments. Later, Chaucer is approached again by the summoner and the pardoner, the gamblers he lost his clothes to earlier. He loses again, and the three approach William because Chaucer has promised William will pay his debt. With payment in hand, Chaucer sends them away, saying, "Be gone. I'm done with you. Except to exact my revenge." They reply, "What on earth could you possibly do to us?" Chaucer says, "I will eviscerate you in fiction—every last pimple, every last character flaw. I was naked for a day; you will be naked for eternity!" This is an allusion to "The Summoner's Tale" and "The Pardoner's Tale" in *The Canterbury Tales*. Chaucer makes these characters look like fools, and we still read these stories today. This is the legacy of writing something down. We've seen summoners and pardoners, even if today we have no idea what those jobs were, as bumbling idiots ever since.

STARTING A NON-PROFIT

One highlight of my career was being a driving force in creating a non-profit for the betterment of cyber security in aviation. A framework in the United States Government called the "National Infrastructure Protection Plan" documents cyber security issues by leveraging an Information Sharing and Analysis Center (ISAC). Like most engineering organizations today, we started out selling the message, primarily in PowerPoint presentations. Good or bad, Microsoft created the PowerPoint chart, and it has really helped many create concise messaging at a high level. A major part of presenting an idea is selling it to senior management. What is typically required at the proposal stage is an effective way to communicate the message that will help convince management to authorize the project. PowerPoint does not do a good job at this. Unfortunately, many still use PowerPoint to document the design and details.

We had a willing audience to listen to us. Cyber security has become a big deal across the board, so everyone agreed with the principle and our cause. To refine the message, we used PowerPoint charts to bring people along. We had willing partners, but no one was convinced to take the next step, essentially putting money down. We had spent a lot of time getting them to that point. I requested that the person running the exercise create a business plan. She did, but it was in PowerPoint—and she resisted writing a document. Her history was in communicating via Power-Point charts. What we were proposing was much bigger than asking for funding for a product development idea or communicating issues found during tests. This was creating a business.

I decided to draft a Word-based business plan. I organized the sections based on the questions people would ask: scope, organization, budget, governance, etc. Then I started to write and fill out all the sections with some text to help document and provide a "straw horse" for others to fill in. After about a week of drafting, I released the document to the team working on the task, and they got it. They moved the thoughts and data from the presentations and added details that couldn't be put into the presentations. Since we were including entities outside of the United States, one of the sensitive parts was the US-centric aspects. It was created using a US government framework and the legal protections around information sharing were based on this and US law. We were incorporating in Delaware and had mostly US-based companies involved upfront. How we documented the international aspects and how we'd operate as an international entity in the plan was critical to bringing on a couple of the big players early on. With help from them and edits provided by them, we documented that aspect in the plan. Prior to getting to this stage, we interviewed many existing ISACs to understand their business models and how to adapt for Aviation. The gold standard was the Financial Services ISAC. While they were US-based, they were international in their outreach, something our organization would be.

The plan completed, the stakeholders understood the details of how we'd function, how the dues would be spent, and growth plans to help sustain the new organization. We formally incorporated and, in several years, had grown to the point where the non-profit was self-sufficient and the recognized leader in cyber security information sharing around the world. We introduced new board members who were non-US and planned for board expansion to provide coverage in all the different regions of the world. This would not have happened if we didn't create the formally documented business plan. Also, in the beginning, we strived to create processes, employee handbooks, business plans, and command media for operating the business. In some respects, our business was functioning much better with more documented processes than some of the other non-profits that had been in business much longer than we had.

AIRPLANE DESIGN

Having worked for the Boeing Company for thirty-five years, I came to realize the power of writing things down, starting with documenting your design. One thing that building a complex machine requires is documenting the design and also the building process. In starting a design, one begins with a plan. Plans of all varieties capture the business aspects, the testing aspects, the procurement strategies, and how the final design will be produced. As the project begins, we document the systems design in a specification. Writing a specification is an art—too much detail and you constrain the supplier; too little and you give the supplier license to build something that may not meet your original intent. Also, since these endeavors are very expensive, attention to detail often becomes a key negotiating point or reason for a cost assertion. I have experienced both over-specifying products and had it come very close to where we intended, only to find a critical flaw that needed to be addressed after testing and reviewing the product. These become cost assertions and can happen on both sides of the contract. I have also been party to a design with minimal description in the specification, but we contractually controlled the supplier's interpretation and final design.

Different thoughts in how to document the design exist. I'll talk about two here on opposite sides of the spectrum, but they capture probably the most used. The first is a "waterfall" design. In this design, one captures everything on the plan and specification for building the product and the documentation is provided to the supplier. While you may spend time working with the supplier and other system interfaces, the premise is capturing all the requirements in a single document. The quality of the design and ultimate build are dependent on your documentation. Since these exercises are often on a higher-level master plan, there is always a schedule demand on the release of this document. While this is a noble plan, it has some critical flaws, one being the demand by all the groups interacting to produce your final release. Some design elements are dependent on others, so not planning for a phased approach will result in rework and potential quality issues during the build—costing time and money. While there may be some issues with a waterfall method, it does provide a clean baseline design, whether it is right or wrong. Having a clear baseline is critical in managing change and resolving issues when they arise.

An alternative is a process called "agile," which is often used in software design. In this process, the design is interactive, and requirements are documented over time as the design progresses. Data shows that the best laid "waterfall" plan always falls short in both schedule and cost. In agile, the idea is to work on the elements required in a phased approach, working between groups to accomplish the task documented in the "program increment." It also leverages the idea of developing parts of the design and then documenting your progress. This is much easier to do in a software development program where you can write the code prior to documenting the requirements, but the principle is the same. By exploring the design between groups working together and understanding the end goal, the thought is you can produce a much better overall design than trying to understand all the elements upfront. Entire businesses exist to teach and certify people on specific processes and frameworks to accomplish tasks with formal roles for people working in an "agile" development program.

Pros and cons exist for each method, and adapting an "agile" method in a large organization can be a challenge. To counter this, we have hybrid models that try to combine the predictability of a waterfall concept with an agile method allowing both a clear baseline and a much more collaborative methodology. The key with both methods is the design is well documented, independent of the methodology.

DOCUMENTING PERFORMANCE

As a manager, we are provided training on all sorts of things from developing people skills to managing performance. When I was promoted to senior manager, it was a significant step. I got to move into a larger office and had much more responsibility. To get a handle on what my new role entailed, I created a structured document that captured the organization and my new role. I started off with the group organization, broke it down to each group's roles and responsibilities, and documented some of the strategic elements I saw in each. Part of the document captured the budgets and our budget sources. I provided it to the last person who had held my position to see if I captured everything, and he said the group was doing some things he wasn't intimately familiar with. I continued with this type of document going forward, renewing it every year, and sharing it with the management team to make sure I not only understood what the group's work statement was, but to capture strategic elements beyond my thoughts. This became a key document I referred to often.

One thing I did every year was sit down with each of my direct employees and write down their accomplishments and high-level understanding of what they were doing. As a third-level manager, I was not exposed to daily work, but had an employee responsible for change routing. She would come to me to ask if it was okay to proceed with some change or idea she had to make the process better. One time, I admitted to her that I didn't really know what she did. I trusted her and promised to become aware of what she did. After all, she was my employee and I needed to provide her support. I scheduled some time to sit down to talk with her. I asked her to bring in examples of her daily work and started asking questions and writing the answers down, making sure my written record was correct from her perspective. During the exchange, I think she learned something new about her job. I kept this record of her tasks and maintained it over time. When I met with other managers of employees doing the same work, I had a detailed description I could refer to, and I found over time that I became very intimate with her work along with all the others in my immediate group.

I did this with all my direct employees. Initially, I had a pretty good idea of what everyone did, but I found by documenting it in writing, I had much more meaningful interactions with them and others in similar positions. As happened with the first employee, many learned they were doing something they had not realized, or we found they were not doing something I thought they were doing. I also found a couple of people I thought could do more, and when I started providing them with more work, I discovered they were much more capable than I thought. This realization was possible because we documented their role together and defined what they were doing. When I retired, I gave these notes to my replacement.

I often had open discussions with my coworkers on strategic plans or problems we were encountering. I had two large whiteboards installed in my office, and we'd sit around drawing pictures and capturing thoughts in real time. We used the whiteboard so everyone could see, and often they would add to the thoughts or get up and draw their own pictures. When done, we'd take a picture of it and transfer the information to a document. We would then circulate the document to others for feedback. I have a directory full of pictures of whiteboards and ideas, strategies, and thoughts. These range from how to accomplish a challenging task to documenting how we were organized. Putting it in writing for all to see was the only clear way to communicate complex ideas, and often, just figuring out how to communicate a complex idea was a complex task. I found these sessions to be the most effective way to clarify and document discussions.

Other reasons for documenting your work abound. A family acquaintance worked in a group home and was often praised for her work. She told me this often. One day, she said she was being disciplined. She was not sure why; she had been praised often and was still being praised, even after that event. I told her to get a notebook and document what she had done during her shift and write down comments from her manager—good and bad. One thing I learned during my time at Boeing was something written has much more relevance than verbal responses, even if it isn't 100 percent accurate. I then asked her to share her notes with her boss in some form, either verbally sharing her notes or sharing the actual notes. She didn't do it. After several months, she was let go. I'm not sure of the specific circumstances, but she challenged the firing because they claimed it was due to poor performance. Had she documented her work and feedback, she might have had a case. Without documentation, it's their word against yours, and she was never able to effectively challenge the firing.

BE CAREFUL WHAT YOU SAY

As with everything, documentation has a good and a bad side. I have focused at a high level on the good aspects of writing things down. What's the negative side? We touched on it earlier—everything written down is captured for all eternity if the document remains available. What is written is up for interpretation and can be contested. With so much emphasis on social media, people are finding things they posted several years ago and beyond have come back to haunt them. A comment from five years ago that was perfectly acceptable in context is available for interpretation and can be brought back up and used out of context very easily. As of this writing, we are seeing an emphasis on equality and ending harassment. Many call it "cancel culture." This idea has people leveraging social and mainstream media to punish and erase anything deemed offensive or that does not support the current understanding of equality and proper behavior. Historical references are being erased and comments made in a less enlightened time are being used to force people from their jobs. Even comedians are having a hard time finding things to make fun of—even the simplest ideas may be interpreted in a negative light.

I often make fun of myself, thinking it is safe, but even that could be risky depending on what I compare myself to or something I comment on that may be considered offensive. Even Dr. Seuss (Theodor Geisel) is not immune. His estate recently chose to retire several books he had written decades ago that included racial stereotypes people no longer find acceptable. With the announcement, many put the retired books up for sale on a web-based commerce platform to take advantage of those who may want to preserve them for posterity (and make some money). The platform has since removed the related posts selling the books. I am not intimate with Dr. Seuss, so while I read his books when I was younger, I really don't have much of an opinion on them. But I honestly believe they were not written with bad intent.

The point is, contradictory to the primary message of this chapter, be careful what you write down. It is permanent and can be used against you. We have many other reasons to be careful about what we put in writing. Early in my career, I was in a presentation where I was providing some design details and thoughts on a problem we had on an airplane. I had put together some good visual aids and started in on my presentation. As I got into the material, one of the executives in the meeting started asking questions—question not based on what I said, but what was on the chart. He was a seasoned engineer and manager and had some insightful questions, questions I was not prepared to answer and questions that were out of context from what I was trying to communicate. Nonetheless, the questions were based on the material I presented, and it soon dawned on me that some of my visual aids showed concepts and ideas that were being taken as fact. He cornered me quickly, and my brilliant presentation collapsed.

After that, I met with my chief engineer to relate my experience. He chuckled a little and said, "All of these executives were once engineers and like to engineer things. As executives, they don't get that opportunity a lot. Your mistake was providing data he could ask questions about. You need to leave the data out and provide concepts that convey the message." It was a brilliant comment and one I often shared.

Some of the best presenters' visual aids do not include the message on the visual aid but include it as part of the verbal presentation. I attended a presentation from one of our vice presidents who had one chart: a timeline of airplanes built. It was probably one of the best presentations I ever saw.

SUMMARY

The written word is extremely powerful, both for good and bad. If used correctly, it can become a historical record. If used incorrectly, it can come back to haunt you. When I was dealing with Mrs. Anderson on the hill, she sent me some very interesting notes, even accusing me of grabbing power in the association in a manner that would make a sitting US senator blush. Reading her message got me a little upset, but on the advice of my brother, I didn't respond in kind. Many of the messages went unanswered, and in those I did answer, I was very careful to avoid emotional responses or say anything misleading or non-factual. I foresaw the day when they might come back to haunt me as a permanent record of my state of mind at the time. Instead, I have a permanent record of her state of mind.

I remember Supreme Court testimony when Brett Kavanaugh was being confirmed. He had claims levied against him from when he was in high school and college, so he pulled out his journal from that time. He is approximately my age, but I don't know of anyone else who kept a journal and recorded daily events at the time, nor do I really know of anyone who does it today. In the end, he was confirmed. I don't know how much that journal came into play, but it did at times challenge the verbal claims, and in my mind, gave more credence to his account of events than the accounts of his accusers.

I'm not suggesting keeping a daily journal, but document significant events in writing. Work events or when you last painted your house could all be helpful in the future. Sooner or later, you'll wonder when you last painted your house and if it's due for another coat. History is made up of written words, symbols, and hieroglyphs. They give us insight into another time sometimes centuries away. Events of today will be studied and analyzed in the future with future generations judging our actions. During the Civil War, Abraham Lincoln was not a popular president, but today, he is looked at as one of our greatest.

Aside from history, the written word is critical for business, contracts, and legal proceedings. Designs for all forms of devices from airplanes to pencil sharpeners need to be documented to build and maintain them. How a proposal is written is probably the key element in getting the job. Documentation is also important in understanding your daily work, and it can help in working with others.

Be careful, though, about what you document and how much you record. Politicians are intimately aware that their history might come back to haunt them during a campaign. Unfortunately, with the rise of and reliance on social media, this phenomenon is starting to affect regular people.

EXERCISES

1. Have you found old letters or even text describing personal events in the past? Have you thought about documenting your story?

    _____

    _____

    _____

    _____

    _____

2. Have you ever been in a strategic session with others? How did they capture the thoughts and ideas?

    _____

    _____

    _____

    _____

    _____

3. Have you thought about how some of your social posts may be inter-
    preted many years in the future?

    _____

    _____

    _____

    _____

CHAPTER 11

RECOGNIZE EVERYONE

"It's not what you do that is important; it is who you work for."

— Sean Sullivan, Chief Engineer Boeing

RECOGNITION

The power of recognition cannot be overstated. If you search the web and look around at events, the world is full of motivational speakers, and many of them stress the importance of recognition. Many very famous people's inspirational words are found online, but a quote that has stuck with me came from an employee of mine who said, "It's not what you do that is important; it is who you work for."

I know of many fun and exciting jobs, but with the wrong leader, they can become miserable. I have seen this firsthand when a new manager comes in and the entire group's energy and performance drop. In extreme cases, you see the group dissolve as people leave for other jobs. Once you have had a poor manager, you understand this dynamic. When I was looking for jobs later in my career, who I worked for became as important as what I did. Also, as a manager, I found myself at times being interviewed by potential candidates and knew that they asked some of my colleagues how it was to work for me. As a manager, you don't do the work; you motivate other people to get the work done, and you can't do that effectively without attracting top talent.

COLIN POWELL

I've attended all sorts of seminars and events where prominent people presented and gave their perspective on the world. A notable one was Colin Powell. At the time, he had just been the Secretary of State for George W. Bush and was relating stories from his tenure there. It was very interesting and provided insight many never understand. Then he talked about recognition. We often tend to look at people through the lens of their job title or role. We usually do not give as much thought to others who seem less significant in our minds. This group may include everyone we deal with, from the server at the restaurant to the valet parking our car.

Secretary Powell told a story about working late one night when the janitor came in to clean up. The janitor, not realizing Powell was working late, stopped short and apologized. He said he would come back later. After all, the Secretary of State was an important person and someone he did not want to disrupt. Powell stopped him and said that while his role was important, the janitor's role was just as important. The Office of Secretary of State represents the United States Government to the world. How it appears and how clean it is reflects directly on the United States of America. The janitor's role in keeping it clean and well-maintained was just as important, if not more important in representing the United States to all who visited the office. When I heard this from Powell, having never thought about it before, I reflected on his words and firmly believed they were true.

Powell then moved on to talk about his interactions with the parking garage attendants. In the parking garage, cars were parked two, three, or four deep. Being inquisitive, he asked the parking lot attendant one day how they decided where to park the cars. The attendant said it was easy—if you say hi, and you are pleasant, your car gets parked in front; if not, it ends up behind others. The attendant told Secretary Powell, "You always say, 'Good morning,' so your car is always in front."

BOEING FACILITIES

Like many large corporations, Boeing has organizations that handle everything from security to sanitation and maintaining the offices. One organization I interacted with frequently was Facilities. Facilities has significant influence on the quality of your work environment and how the office is arranged. As new programs came online, Facilities had to find places for the new program employees, and those programs often desired a central location. This resulted in groups moving frequently within buildings, from building to building, or even to different sites in the area. The result could be a much better work arrangement or something much worse than you had.

I worked with Facilities on all manner of things—safety, evacuation checklists, cleaning, and updates. When we moved into the building, it needed a fresh coat of paint and new floor coverings. The carpets were replaced before we moved in. With temporary cubicles, getting this done before the layouts were complete was critical. The next item was painting of the walls. The building was divided into six large bays with two east-west hallways and three north-south hallways. A decision was made to paint about half the building, which included the hallways and two bays. This building was probably built in the 1970s, and we weren't sure when it had been painted last. We put in a request to have our bay painted, as well, but we were told it wasn't in that year's budget, which meant we probably wouldn't get it painted for quite some time. After you've moved in, it's much more difficult to get things like this done.

At Boeing, we had a simple recognition system with varying levels of awards. There were cash awards at the top for significant events and "points" that could be traded for merchandise. These were both formal systems that a manager or executive would have to approve. The other recognition awards were plastic coins good for free ice cream, $3, or $5 that could be used in the cafeterias. These could be handed out to people on the spot and did not require any real approval short of a manager ordering them. They also came out of a higher-level budget, so getting them was not a budgetary issue like most things in a company of Boeing's size. My office administrator Lisa made it a point to get a lot of these coins and pass them out to the staff regularly. Lisa also started to give them out to all the support people and thanked them for all their hard work. I had given up on getting the walls painted, but she hadn't. She had a relationship with pretty much all the different organizations that supported us and only got me involved when an approval was needed or an issue arose. I felt like Colonel Henry Blake from M.A.S.H. at times, just approving items without really knowing what they were. I trusted Lisa and this was her responsibility, so I didn't see the need to review this stuff in detail.

Lisa made it her task to get the walls painted. She started to feed the lower-level Facilities people these coins and then started meeting with their managers, praising their work, and providing these coins to them as well. Lo and behold, one day Lisa came into my office and asked what color I wanted the walls painted. Lisa had convinced them to paint our bay— they had found the funds in the budget. Our bay was painted, and I found out later that they decided not to paint a bay they had planned to, saying ours was in more need. I don't think that was the real reason. I think they appreciated people thanking them and providing small gestures of gratitude to reenforce the thought. Seeing this success, I recognized Lisa formally, and we decided we were going to praise all the support staff and provide positive feedback. It was amazing how the mailroom started to call us right away when we had packages to pick up instead of waiting, and the service we got from the cleaning folks was great. These folks only got negative feedback, so giving them praise had a really powerful effect on our group and their support of it.

Everyone dreaded meeting with Facilities about space allocation. Every group had an allocation with some spare desks for summer interns or new staff. When these were gone, getting space was very difficult, and if critical, it could result in a move to another location, something nobody liked. I was about to have my first meeting with Rebecca, the Facilities manager responsible for our plant, and Lisa warned me Rebecca meant business. We set up a meeting in my office and sat down with Rebecca. When she came in, we saw she was professionally dressed and more for- mal than expected. I could immediately tell she was ready for battle.

Rebecca had a reputation and often got into terse discussions with the managers and employees managing the different buildings about reallo- cating their unused space. She put down a map of the desks in the build- ing with all the empty desks in my area highlighted. I had a large group so it spanned two bays, and she had both bays highlighted. The map showed desks scattered throughout the bays, none of them really together in a group. Rebecca started off by telling me she was going to have to take all of the empty desks. Her voice was stern and commanding, with no opening for compromise. She had done this before and making her first offer extreme, helped in the negotiations.

Sitting there, I thought about Facilities painting our bays and the support we got, and decided to take another tact. I said okay, and did not argue with her. This caught Rebecca off guard, and she asked me to repeat what I had said. I said again, "Okay. We're not using them, and I understand you need the space." At that moment, Rebecca deflated and went from a very rigid, formal stance to very relaxed.

"I know you want the desks in this bay, but if you move my folks over from the other bay and fill in these spaces, you'd have even more space," I said.

Rebecca looked at the map and started to smile. "You're right," she said. She thanked me and went into some detail about how difficult it usually is to work these things out with managers. Most didn't respect her. In the end, she usually got what she asked for, but only after a long, drawn-out battle.

We filled out the hour talking about other things, including some personal background from all of us. I didn't fully realize it at the time, but I had just made a significant ally. Rebecca had much more power than I gave her credit for initially and ended up in charge of wholesale building moves. She did move my group around, but going forward, she protected us from these big moves, and in the five years we were in the building, we were probably the only group that never had to move. Rebecca always moved people around us. She would come and ask me for help regularly. Having been in the company for more than twenty-five years at that point, I knew almost everyone, and I became her key sponsor and helped change her reputation with as many managers as I could. She told me once that a couple of managers I talked to started getting along with her better, and as a result, she was trying to help them with their facilities issues more proactively. The managers noticed this.

THE YEARLY SURVEY

At Boeing, we held a yearly survey that gave employees a means of providing feedback in a neutral way. The survey asked all sorts of questions to measure how well employees liked their managers and executive management, how good down flow of information was being handled, etc. A key part of this survey was recognition—do you feel recognized for the job you are doing? After the survey, we shared the results and comments with the group and decided on a few items we would work on based on the survey results. We picked things we could actually change that mattered to our people and filtered out the global issues—parking, pay, and other items that were not in our local control.

One year, I decided to work on my recognition score. My group's results were pretty good, higher than average, so I was happy. While the recognition score was not bad, I thought it would be something we could work on to get real results. I met with my managers, and we laid out a plan. First, we would be very proactive with formal recognition and start a process to drive more formal recognition in the group. Second, because recognition is not just a top-down activity, I really wanted to encourage employees to recognize each other. We made sure employees were recognized in the formal awards, but we also used coins and other less formal recognition tokens available to us. In one meeting, I handed out a small recognition award to everyone and told them they could not keep it but had to recognize someone else. I thought it would help kickstart more of this activity in the group. It was interesting to see how it progressed.

We did this aggressively for a year and waited for the new survey results. When they came out, I was shocked—our score actually went down. How could this be with all the focus on getting "things" out to the group to recognize them? After some reflection, it dawned on me that recognition is much more than tokens, and a simple thank you in front of others or in private (depending on the person) was much more effective. Passing out trinkets and free lunches wasn't necessarily genuine, and people can see right through that. I decided that, going forward, I would still provide formal recognition, but would try to go out of my way to talk to people on the floor and thank them personally for their daily work, even if the daily work was a little late. A lot of work is much more difficult than initially thought, and even if late, it was an accomplishment that needed to be recognized rather than scolded. This recognition gets into empathy and understanding the challenges the group faced to let them know you understand their situation—something that requires a lot of daily interaction.

THE SUMMER PICNIC

One year, we decided to host a summer picnic for the group. Group picnics were usually held in a parking lot on Boeing property where people could leave their desks for thirty to sixty minutes, have lunch, and then go back to work. We decided something offsite would be much more rewarding, so we hosted a picnic in Mukilteo at a state park near the water. We estimated how many people would come and purchased pizza and drinks for the occasion. To our surprise, the entire group showed up, and we were short on pizza. Then the smaller team in Renton (about forty miles south) noticed they were not included, so we hosted a second picnic, but this time we had it catered at the local park near the plant on the south shore of Lake Washington. This one went much better—we ordered enough food, knowing the turnout would be good.

These two events were a huge success, so we decided to do it again. Talking with the management team, one of the new managers said they hosted an annual picnic on Lake Washington for the entire group and held it in the middle between Everett and Renton, so all could get together. It sounded like a plan, so we started to research the best place and best time to do this. We decided to pick Mercer Island, the park on the lid, and picked Seafair week. Seafair is an annual event hosted by Seattle which includes navy ships, hydroplane races, and the Blue Angels. Being on Mercer Island, it would be a short walk to the Interstate 90 bridges to view the races and the Blue Angels (they closed I-90 during the practices). Also, it was always nice on that weekend. That would be our new plan, and we would have it catered. We also decided not only to include my group of around 150, but all the people who worked on the platforms. This brought the number to around 300.

Getting to Mercer Island from both sites and later the Boeing field site was not a simple task. At the time, when the I-90 bridge was closed, you could only get to the site from the east side. If you left early, you would be away from work longer, and with the events, you would stay at the picnic longer. This makes it an overhead charging issue and something I always had to battle with my bosses about, but we proceeded that first year, a little nervous about how successful it would be. We estimated around 150 would show up but ordered food for 200. To our surprise, about 200 showed up. It was a great success, and many thanked me for arranging for the Blue Angels to give a show for us during the picnic. We had all the cabin systems folks at the event, and it was great to see them all together. I still had a funding issue, but we figured out how to handle that. Over time, I realized this one event really helped the team bond, and we got much more work out the folks than the few hours of time lost during the event.

This became the famous "Cabin Systems Picnic," and everyone in airplane systems heard about it. After the first year, in a meeting with my peers, I showed pictures, and I think they were all jealous. When they looked into a similar event, they would call and ask how I handled the funding. I was not really forthright with them, and most didn't want to take the risk. A few years later, the decision was made to stop funding these types of events. We decided to press on anyway. Instead of hiring a local caterer, we would bring grills and do it ourselves. The first year we did it, everyone was aware of the new policy and asked who would cater it. I told everyone we had a very exclusive caterer, but we would have to charge $5 per person for the event. When some complained, I replied, "You don't need to have our lunch; you can bring your own, but please show up." That year, Lisa, my office administrator, had hats and BBQ aprons made up—JAC BBQ (that's me!). Everyone loved it, and we were actually approached by others on the island about how to contact us for events. This continued until I left Boeing, and at the peak, we had 350 people attending. People looked forward to it every year. One year, I had a new boss, who found out about it about two weeks before the event. He was not happy that a group of his was hosting, about how we funded it, or about how people would get there. I told him I'd cancel if he told me to. After some thought, he backed off and let it proceed. The next week when the charges came in, he didn't challenge the overages.

We had people who would take a day of vacation to attend all day. The standing joke and something I'd announce before the event was how I contacted the Blue Angels to invite them, and they had confirmed for the year. One year, I was transferred to the 777 program and was no longer the cabin systems chief, so I was no longer the host for the party. It was also a year when, for some reason, the Blue Angels did not come to Seafair. A year later, I was back in charge of cabin systems and apologized for not getting the Blue Angels lined up while I was away. That year they returned. This went on for fifteen years and reaped unexpected rewards over time.

One Sunday, I was near the Everett plant and thought I'd check out a 777 airplane on which we had just installed a brand-new satellite communications system. It was high-bandwidth internet for the cabin and the first installation on a large commercial jet. It was a pretty significant change for Boeing and the industry. I had spent a lot of time on the flight line during my early years, but as the chief of cabin systems, I did not really wander out to the airplane much anymore. I was not sure of the new protocols, etc. I called up JJ, the field engineer who worked on the platform, and asked about the protocols. He lived close by and said to hold up for a minute and he would come out to take me on a tour. Sure enough, he showed up, took me into the doghouse near the airplane, and introduced me to everyone. He then took me onto the airplane with a flight line technician to go over the system. It was a first-class tour and demo of the new system. While we were on the plane, his boss showed up and was surprised he was there. JJ said I called and needed help. His boss looked at both of us in an interesting way and left. I asked JJ, "What is going on?" He said his boss had called him just before me asking to meet him on the airplane, and JJ said he could not. I was a little honored he came out for me. He did not work for me, and I really did not have any connection to him other than the picnic. That event gave me special status with the group and, I realized later, a lot of others. I believe it was a key reason JJ went out of his way to help me.

SUMMARY

I do not think we truly appreciate the people who help us, serve us, or support us. From where our car gets parked to service at a restaurant, we depend on people, people who can go out of their way to provide great service or ignore you. The CEO for the Boeing Commercial Airplane Company once said, "Airlines don't buy airplanes, people do." He gave credit for one airline sticking with Boeing products during hard times solely based on his personal relationship with the CEO. Working with suppliers, airlines, and industry folks boils down to personal relationships. With a positive, trusting relationship, you can find out what is really going on or you may get a call asking for help with something. Part of maintaining good relationships is recognizing people and their value.

I have a ritual where I go out to breakfast every Saturday. I sit in the bar and have gotten to know the bartender Terry very well. (She is the waitress for the bar as well.) I started leaving exceptionally large tips. For a $12 meal, I would leave $20. She noticed. When I come in, she has my drinks ready and knows pretty much what I'm going to eat. She'll come by and chat and will always make sure I have everything I need. On one occasion, we were talking and one of the other patrons at the bar was trying to get her attention. I told Terry, and she looked behind her and then looked back at me and said, "He can wait—he's a cheap SOB." Another time I took Bonnie in, and it was very busy. Terry said the kitchen was slammed, and it would probably be forty minutes before we got our meals. I said no problem, and we ordered. The order came out very quickly, not even close to forty minutes, and I said, "That was quick." Terry said, with a grin, "I kind of moved your order up." I tip well everywhere I go, especially places I frequent. In the grand scheme of things, it is not really a lot of money and something I can afford. I once worked in the service industry—a little more in the tip jar really helped back then.

Recognizing people and respecting them should be second nature. When you talk to someone, you should use positive comments, not negative ones. I think it's easier for people to look at the negative side of things, and if you are one of those people, I would suggest you work on turning that around. I used to be one of those negative people. On one occasion, I ran into my friend's daughter who had just gotten a job in the coffee stand at Boeing. She was excited to see me. I said, "Looks like they are hitting the bottom of the barrel." She looked at me and said, "I'm sorry. I missed that." I thought, *Why did I say that?* I just wanted to acknowledge she was there in a new job, and while my comment was a joke, I should not have said it. I quickly responded, "I see they have pulled out the A team." Her face broke into a big smile, and I felt better saying it. After that day, I really try to make positive statements, not negative ones in these situations. The result is always better.

EXERCISES

1. When was the last time you thanked someone for service they pro-

vided? Was it a significant help or something simple? Do you provide positive feedback, even if it was not the best service?

_____

_____

_____

_____

2. Do you have trusting relationships you leverage to accomplish tasks or get information? How do you think these developed?

_____

_____

_____

_____

3. Think of a time when you had poor service or had a negative meeting with someone. Could you have said or done something to change to a more positive one?

_____

_____

_____

_____

CHAPTER 12

HELPING OTHERS

"The best way to find yourself is to lose yourself in the service of others."

— Mahatma Gandhi

IT'S A DOG-EAT-DOG WORLD

Abraham Maslow was an American psychologist and philosopher known for "Maslow's Hierarchy of Needs" published in 1943. Over the years, many have studied these needs and some critics claim he got it wrong. I think, though, his hierarchy holds some basic truths about who we are. Maslow's Hierarchy of Needs has five levels, listed below and starting with the most basic:

- Physiological needs—food, water, etc.

- Safety needs—security, safety, etc.

- Belongingness and love needs—friendships, intimacy

- Esteem needs—feeling of accomplishment

- Self-Actualization—achieving one's full potential

Looking at our social structure, I see how different social classes may be at one level working toward the next. The person on the street may just be looking for something to eat and a safe place to stay. Others may keep to themselves or be working in jobs to get ahead. While you can argue that people could have elements of being at all levels, those near the bottom of the pyramid are more likely to worry about themselves and how to advance their current reality. Those at the top may have the same mentality in a quest to further their self-esteem and creative activities. In looking at social media platforms, I would say their purpose is primarily to build up the esteem of the person publishing material or to sell a service that will help the merchant or vendor advance their cause. One exception is the "Go Fund Me" site where there is an element of helping others.

My uncle was somewhat self-centered in his view of others outside his family. I remember once when I was young, he left a minimal tip and somewhat chastised my father for leaving one he thought was too large. His comment was "Save it for you kids." I remembered that when I was working in the food service industry during high school where the bulk of your salary is from tips. I have a different perspective. I will generally give more, and as I commented before, it often results in much better service going forward.

Everyone needs help; it can be in the form of money, advice, or even getting a task completed. I often went into downtown Seattle when I first moved there, and I loved to talk to the people on the street. These people were down on their luck. Just talking to them in an honest fashion really gave them a way to express their frustrations. On one occasion, we parked on a side street with plans to head into a local bar. Getting out of the car, we saw two individuals sitting on the curb. I made a wisecrack to them to make sure nobody stole my hubcaps. (Funny since I didn't have any.) One of them said, "You too good to have a drink with us?" I decided to sit down with them, have a drink, and talk to them while the rest of my friends went into the bar. I sat with them for over an hour, and they told me a story of losing their jobs fishing and how tough it had been since. One told me he knew of a great fishing hole and would love to take me to it. I listened and was myself, not pretending to understand fully their situation, but expressing my opinions on the situation. These were normal guys who were down on their luck. After I left them, I joined my friends in the bar. When I returned to my car, there was a note on my windshield thanking me for taking the time to listen to them and treating them with respect. I still have the note.

Another time I gave a man $100 to go shopping. I didn't follow him into the store, but I watched from outside to see what he purchased—diapers, laundry soap, and other household items. I'm not sure why I did it, but I told him to help someone else in need when he could. Another time, I purchased a train ticket for a guy from Portland. He was beaten up but didn't seem like a typical street person. He had come to Seattle for a job and didn't end up getting it. That night, he was robbed and had all of his money taken, effectively stranding him in Seattle. I told him the same thing—he needed to help someone else. The movie *Pay It Forward* shows how powerful this action can be. Helping someone doesn't take money or some big effort. Sometimes just talking to someone and helping them feel better about themselves or encouraging them to take the next step can be just as powerful. I don't really spend time in Seattle doing this anymore, but when I started doing it, it became infectious, and I often recall some of the foolish (as my friends relayed to me at the time) things I did. The people I interacted with were in a place where just a kind voice or inclusion in a minor activity was uplifting for them—and me.

INTERACTIONS ON A PERSONAL LEVEL

The value of making your interactions with others personal cannot be overstated. Forgive me if I repeat some of what I've said previously, but you need to make sure those you are talking to or helping know you are listening and fully engaged. We have all had the boss, parent, or elder who did not really engage. Yes, they listened, but you knew they really did not care or absorb what you were saying. Over time, you minimized your interactions and only went to them when you had to. If you had a pressing need, they might not have been the first person you reached out to. We talked earlier about my experience with Dr. Phil's advice on how you interact with people. That extended to the group level and how your group or company is perceived by others. Many groups and companies that do not fully embrace interacting at a personal level flounder and fail.

As a manager, I had a habit of walking the floor. When I first became a manager, I was somewhat young compared to those I was managing, and a few engineers intimidated me a little. In walking the floor, I ran into one of these engineers. I decided to start a conversation with him. It wasn't about work or what he was doing, just some questions about his family and his interests. We talked for several minutes, and I found out he was probably just as intimidated by me as I was by him. By interacting on a personal level, we established some common ground and understanding. Over time, I tried to reach out to everyone on the floor, walking the floor once a day, sometimes taking thirty minutes to an hour just talking to the team informally. What I discovered was I was building trust and a camaraderie that came in handy when a critical task needed to be taken care of. I'm not saying everyone was thrilled about my stories, but I truly believe everyone felt I was approachable.

APPROACHABLE

As a leader, one of the hardest things to do is create an atmosphere where you are approachable. As I was promoted to manager, senior manager, and director, I found that those I thought I had a good relationship with were alienated by my new title. I had a woman who worked for me as a manager with whom I had a pretty close working relationship. I left the job and took another. A year went by and I was promoted into an executive position back in the same group. That same woman treated me differently. She was afraid to talk to me, and she didn't really engage me when I walked the floor. It took some time, but I slowly got back to the same relationship. You can't underestimate the power of a title.

As you progress up the food chain, you lose contact with people due to the size of your group. The company Gore-Tex found that factories with more than 150 people did not run as smoothly as those with less. They decided to limit the number of people in a factory to 150. Malcolm Gladwell's book *The Tipping Point* talks about the Gore-Tex management structure and discusses "Dunbar's Number," attributed to Robin Dunbar. Dunbar claims that 150 people is the point where members of any social group lose their ability to function effectively in social relationships. His research indicates you have:

- Five intimate friends

- Fifteen good friends (including the five intimate ones)

- Fifty friends (including the good and the intimate)

- A hundred and fifty acquaintances (all encompassing)

This number is highlighted in history as well. Neolithic farming communities tended to split after growing to around 150 people. Roman military units were approximately 150 in size with modern armies similarly divided. Thinking about myself, when I was a senior manager, I had about 150 people reporting to me, and I had a pretty good rapport with almost all of them. I had a weekly group meeting everyone was invited to and that most attended at least once a month. When I moved to the executive level, that number became 450 to 500, and I noticed I was no longer able to maintain the same level of intimacy with group members. While I tried, a key to my success with the large group was how they perceived me. I had to avoid showing favoritism, have an open-door policy I actually adhered to, and interact with enough people to show everyone that I was open to discussions. I believe, over time, I was successful, but it took work and time.

EVERYONE HAS A PLACE

One of the most important things I learned in my many years is there is a job or place for everyone—you just need to find it. I recruited at colleges, and after many years, I realized the students didn't really know what they wanted to do when they graduated. Many would come up to the booth and tell me how excited they would be to work for Boeing, but after a few questions, it was clear not many really knew what they would be doing. Looking at my career, I earned a Bachelor of Science in Electrical Engineering with a focus in electrical power and electromagnetic energy. At Boeing, while I hired into the electrical power group on the commercial airplane side, what I was doing a year later really had nothing to do with electrical power or electromagnetic energy. In the end, I was heavy into networking and cyber security. I also went into management. I found a path and job I enjoyed as a manager. It became my responsibility to find the right job for my employees—something I learned the hard way.

Josh was a technical employee who had a significant role in our group. He was responsible for reviewing technical data from suppliers similar to several others in the group, only he didn't really seem to perform. I was not impressed with his work, and in reviews, he didn't rank as well as others. He wasn't happy, and it was apparent when you talked to him. I was new to management and didn't really pay much attention to him, but when he announced he had a new job, I was somewhat relieved. He was moving into more of a test and technical role working in product development. A few years later, when we were moving into wireless connectivity, he surfaced again, not as an employee reviewing technical data, but an expert in wireless communication, something he really enjoyed and succeeded at. I was shocked, but it dawned on me that I hadn't really understood he had needed to find a new role in the group. After that event, I would go out of my way to find out if employees were happy, and if not, if I could find a different role that would help. In one of my MBA classes, a mentor told a story about how they promoted someone before they were ready, and they were not performing. He was going to replace the person; it was sad because, while the person had potential, by moving him up too fast, he would probably never reach that level again. If they had matured him and waited, he could have gone farther. My mentor told me he was half-responsible for the failure. He had put the person in a position he was not ready for. The other half of the responsibility was on the employee. The lesson here was, as a manager and leader of people, you are, to a certain level, responsible for the success and failure of everyone in the group. When promoting or putting people in charge of projects, you need to make sure they are ready and have the support to ensure they are successful—something easier said than done.

JOB TITLE VS. JOB

Another lesson my mentor taught me related to his daughter. She had just graduated from college and was targeting a very prestigious job with an impressive title. She worked hard for the interview, researched the company, and got the job. Once in the job, she started questioning if she really wanted to be there or was just into the prestige of having it. She soon left the company and moved on to a job she enjoyed.

I often met people who were focused on the job title instead of the job and went to extreme lengths to keep the title, even if it meant less pay or, in a couple of cases, a layoff when the role was terminated, even if a role without the title was offered at the same pay and benefit level. These are probably the most difficult situations to deal with and require honest discussions and listening skills. You have to understand people's motivation and how to move them into roles they truly enjoy, even if it doesn't have the title. Sometimes, there was a cultural element; other times, it was the individual. In either case, it was difficult to navigate.

The importance of a good manager cannot be overstated. A good manager will work with you and help you succeed. The manager will protect you from the nonsense coming from above and take risks in adapting your direction where it makes sense. Part of everyone's role is to seek out those who will help, and your direct superior is where it starts.

SUMMARY

Helping people is something we should all strive for. I truly believe that what you give, you receive back multiple times. Helping can be as simple as donating to charity, just sitting down to talk to someone who is down on their luck, or giving life advice to those just starting out. We all have experiences we would do differently if we could do them over, knowing what we now know. At work, I would always strive to talk to anyone about their career and how to navigate it. I now give advice to others about career moves. Every decision has a consequence, either good or bad. Knowing the implications of a decision is critical to avoiding some of the pitfalls you may fall into along the way. Help can be anything, including financial advice. I wish I had reached out for financial help earlier. In my later years, I learned about different investment options that probably would have been better had I started earlier.

Part of helping others is making them a priority and dedicating your full attention when interacting with them. The key to this is building the perception that you are approachable and know the dynamics of a large organization. Whether at home or at work, people are depending on you, no matter what your role is, and finding time to focus on them will help you become successful. When building a simple structure, investing, parenting, or some other activity, reaching out to others who have been there will make the task much easier and more successful. Doing that requires others to "help you," and when it's your turn, you need to help others in the same manner.

EXERCISES

1. Have you ever gone out of your way to help someone? Describe the situation and how it ended up.

   _____

   _____

   _____

   _____

   _____

   _____

2. Take account of your intimate friends, friends, and acquaintances. Does the 150 number sound reasonable? Do you have more Facebook friends than 150? Would you count all as acquaintances? (book designer put 3-line spaces in)

   _____

   _____

   _____

   _____

   _____

   _____

   _____

3. Did you ever think about your job and realize it wasn't really what you wanted? Did you look for help in changing it or look for a new role?

    _____

    _____

    _____

    _____

    _____

    _____

4. Have you met someone who was more focused on their title or position than their job? Do you think they were successful or happy?

    _____

    _____

    _____

    _____

    _____

    _____

CHAPTER 13

NOT ALL QUESTIONS ARE GOOD QUESTIONS

"I used to think I knew all the answers. Then I thought I knew maybe a few of the answers. Now I'm not even sure I understand the questions. Nobody knows anything."

— Pete Nelson, *I Thought You Were Dead*

"Sometimes the questions are complicated, and the answers are simple."

— Dr. Seuss

MANAGING THE DISCUSSION

We have all been in a situation where someone starts asking a question, it becomes overly complex, and by the end, we're not sure what the real question is. Then there are the simplistic yet obvious questions like, "Why is traffic or parking so bad?" Then there are the late comers to the meeting who arrive just after their questions are answered and you need to repeat the answers for them.

We've been told there are no bad questions, but I would challenge that. Some questions should never be asked, and some answers are so obvious that you wonder why someone would ask in the first place. In either case, as a leader, how you address these questions at home and at work reflects on you and others' perception of you. I recently had an old friend call me. I knew him well in high school, but after college, we drifted apart. He got into trouble and spent some time at the crowbar motel for some minor offenses. About thirty years later, he called out of the blue. He was glad to talk to me and look back on his life, mostly the poor choices he had made. He congratulated me on my life and wished he could have done better.

In the middle of this conversation, he said, "I'm not as smart as you are. I'm stupid." I chuckled a little and said, "You're not stupid. You just don't have very good common sense." He laughed and said, "Thanks. You were always nice to me, but I'm stupid; don't sugarcoat it for me."

The conversation moved on, but I think one reason he talked to me was how I managed the conversation. I didn't let him go down the self-pity hole and tried to keep the conversation positive.

In a meeting, the same holds true. Someone will always ask questions that have no answer or are out of context. Your job, either as the leader of the meeting or a participant, is to acknowledge the question and move on. Respect—that is the key.

You may also find, as I have many times, that the question you thought was irrelevant actually was relevant. By acknowledging it early, you leave the door open to discuss it if the discussion moves in that direction—and it may. Part of acknowledging what you may think is a poor question is also acknowledging that you may not understand the question. In doing this, you become someone people actually look forward to having meetings with or to have lead them.

Perspectives are also a very important thing. At Boeing, we would have a new crop of summer interns every year, which was something we looked forward to. What do you have a new intern do? The joke was to give them a whole bunch of specifications or documents to read. We did this. We didn't really know how to get the interns into the workflow right away.

One individual came in and was given a problem we had been struggling to resolve on an in-service airplane for many years. It was not a significant problem, but something the airline wanted fixed. We asked our new intern to look at it as a way to get him started. We didn't think he would figure it out, but he did. Turns out, he had just completed some classes that focused on engineering challenges for high-rise buildings, and this problem fit right into what he had just learned in school. He knew nothing about airplanes or airplane systems and didn't have any biases like most of the engineers who had been designing and working on them. He took a fresh look from a different perspective and was able to resolve the problem. Never discount those who may not have a deep background in your issue. They may have insights you don't realize.

STAY ON MESSAGE

One of the most important things to do is stay on message. Sharing your views and knowledge with people is an inherently human trait. But in doing so, you really need to make sure you are talking at the right level of detail and keep your comments brief. At work, not doing this can quickly get you into trouble. Bosses don't really want to know the details—they want to know you know the details and will accomplish the task. Most don't need the details of what you are doing; they have enough to worry about with their own daily work.

At Boeing, we had to report our performance every week, and we had a scheduler do these reports. The release of the reports was important and missing dates could cause other groups to fall behind on their milestones, so if you were going to miss a date, you needed to alert the bosses and give them a plan for how you would address the situation. In a discussion like this, if you caused the boss to doubt you, they would start asking detailed questions about your plan and push to have you expedite the work.

All the deliverables included challenges in completing them, but for the most part, we met the dates. The problem we ended up having was our scheduler was sharing to much detail on the daily activity and causing the bosses to doubt our ability to meet the deadlines. When I was called into a meeting to explain, I listened, then turned to the bosses and said, "It will be done on time." That is all they wanted to hear, and based on my track record, they didn't doubt it. When I had a problem, I would speak up, and they knew it. After a couple of meetings like this, I coached the scheduler just to give the high-level detail and leave out the random daily drama. Our reports became short and to the point.

Another key skill is what we used to call the elevator speech. The scenario is you have just entered an elevator with a celebrity or boss you're trying to make a positive impression on. You have from the second floor to the eighth to give them the message—one they will remember. This is a hard one, and you really need to be quick on your feet, but it is a skill everyone should master. You need to formulate your response quickly and get right to the point. If the message requires follow-up, you want the message to compel the person to want to hear more later. We taught people two main things about an elevator speech:

- The three Bs—be brief, be brilliant, and be gone.

- Tell them what you're going to tell them, tell them, and tell them what you told them.

In media training, these messages were reenforced. I had the opportunity to get training from a professional media person. She had done several interviews and relayed some very interesting things. She started out by asking me some questions and taping my responses. At the end, she said, "Do you have any questions for me?" I said no.

Then we reviewed the tape. During the interview, I was in a very relaxed state, leaning back in my chair, answering the questions probably more completely than I should have, and when she asked if I had any closing questions, I didn't respond. She also showed me where she got me to say things she wanted me to say, and after she pointed it out, I started to see the technique being used all the time on TV interviews. For example, she would ask, "So, you forgot the details?" and I would more than likely answer, "Yes, I forgot the details." In a hostile interview, this could be taken out of context. She gave me some tactics to avoid falling into this trap. One was to ask a question in return or not answer the question asked, but answer with your intended message.

Also the proper answer to the details question is, "Details are important, and we are focused on assuring everything is addressed."

The final thing media training focused on was messaging. Always summarize what you've said at the end of the interview. In a lot of interviews or presentations, the last thing you say is what the audience remembers.

When she asked if I had any questions for her at the end of my interview, I didn't have to ask a question, but I had an opportunity to briefly state my message. This is where the elevator speech comes in, and often when you're preparing for a presentation or an interview, you know what the subject will be and should prepare your final "elevator speech."

KNOW WHEN TO BE QUIET

So far in this chapter, we discussed understanding what a meeting or discussion is about. Then we discussed keeping on message. Now we will discuss the final and probably most important part—knowing when to be quiet. This is true everywhere. I've been pulled over for speeding many times, and early on, when I was asked if I knew how fast I was going, if I was going seventy in a fifty-five, I'd say, "I was only going sixty." I had just admitted to speeding, something a judge reminded me of. A law professor at Regent University School of Law, James Duane, has an excellent video called "Don't Talk to the Police." It describes why you need to exercise your Fifth Amendment rights when talking to the police. Anything you say to the police can be used against you; nothing can help you.

Another example of not saying too much is taking oral exams. Anyone who has taken an oral exam can relate to the stress of taking one. In an oral exam, I answered a question correctly and waited for the next question. In the moments after my answer, I filled the awkward pause by elaborating on my answer, which my professor let me do. He then used this as an opening to ask me more questions and found that, while I got the answer correct, I didn't really understand why. Had I not said anything else, I would have been fine. After the exam, he told me, "Only answer the question asked."

I had a boss who did the same thing. He would ask a question, and after you answered, he would pause. In the moment, you would be tempted to keep talking, but you soon learned just to answer the question and shut up.

This also comes into play when you're presenting in a meeting. Presenting is an art. It can take time to learn how to adapt your message to your audience. Presentations for technical employees may need to be detailed while the same presentation to vice presidents may need to be summarized. However, I have watched people present high-level detail to technical employees and lose credibility. Others I've seen go into too much detail with vice presidents and lose their interest or talk over their heads so their audience loses the message. Over time, neither audience will want to hear from you. If a vice president loses interest in your presentations, it could affect your career.

I learned this personally when I presented to a group of senior executives as a manager. You may remember this story from an earlier chapter. I put a lot of detail into the presentation, and once I started, they started asking detailed questions about the material, questions I couldn't answer. I failed in that presentation. I went back to my boss and asked what I had done wrong. He looked at my presentation, and said, "Your problem is you gave them design details. They all used to be engineers and love to revert when they can. What you should have done is present the message without any detail. By doing that, you don't really give them an opportunity to ask detailed questions on your material." After that, I kept design details, for the most part, out of my presentations and was quite successful at presenting in the future.

SUMMARY

At home with your family, in social settings, and at work, questions and answers are basic interaction. The key to success in these interactions is following three simple steps:

1. *Manage the Discussion*—If you're in a work setting, you don't need to elaborate on a personal matter. If you're in a social setting, work matters probably aren't relevant. It may be wise to avoid certain topics and learn ways to deflect some of those discussions.

2. *Stay on Message*—Ensuring your message or discussions are focused is important everywhere. At work, your message needs to be crafted for the audience; at home, your message needs to be targeted at the audience as well. You talk to small children very differently than you talk to older ones.

3. *Know When to Be Quiet*—This is probably the most important point and something we all need to work on. We all have a friend who talks too much, and when they start, we may tune out. You want to be someone people want to hear. A commercial from the 1970s highlighted this idea—"When EF Hutton talks, people listen." In the commercial, when the investor says, "My broker is EF Hutton, and EF Hutton says..." the entire restaurant or gathering gets quiet to listen. You want to be EF Hutton.

Learning how to manage discussions and present to different audiences is a skill you acquire over time. I learned by watching people in meetings and noting how they read the audience. I also had mentors and leaders who gave me feedback on my presentations. Formal training is also an option, but I found watching others and taking notes worked best.

EXERCISES

1. Pay attention to people presenting or media clips. Write down what you think is effective and why.

    _____

    _____

    _____

    _____

2. Have you ever caught yourself talking too much or not answering questions directly? What would the difference be if you said less?

    _____

    _____

    _____

    _____

3. Have you had an opportunity to give an "elevator speech?" How did it go?

    _____

    _____

    _____

    _____

CHAPTER 14

CLIMBING THE LADDER

"It's not whether you get knocked down; it's whether you get up."

— Vince Lombardi

WHAT DO YOU WANT TO DO WHEN YOU GROW UP?

Part of the fun of my job at Boeing was recruiting, especially at my alma mater, Montana State University. I participated in the Electrical and Computing Engineering Advisory Board and spent time on campus talking to students. Talking to them and looking back at myself at that age, I realized a few things. First, most didn't really know what they wanted to do, and second, they just wanted a good paying job with opportunities. Now, that may not be true for all the candidates. People in the military and older students with work experience had some life experience that helped guide them, but even then, I found a little vagueness when I talked to them.

Working for a large company like Boeing made it easy for me to talk to students. I represented a commercial airplane company and could discuss the many different jobs available—and those that weren't. For example, my group didn't do detailed circuit design, but somewhere in Boeing, we did, and if someone really wanted to go down that path, we could direct them to the right department.

I was also pretty blunt with students. I often said they probably didn't know what they really wanted to do and told them that in three to five years, technology would change and the opportunities would be different. When I graduated, I wanted to focus on electrical power and electromagnetic energy. This simplistic goal had me headed toward a power company or something in wireless communication. I had offers. One was good, with a governmental power provider, but the pay was almost half what others offered. At that time, money meant more to me than the specific job, and I ended up taking a position at Boeing working in the electrical power group for a new airplane called the 7J7. It wasn't long before I stopped working electrical power stuff and got more into digital design. The electromagnetic focus I had in school was helpful, but it really didn't have a lot of relevance in my daily job other than understanding the importance of it when designing systems.

As my career progressed, I moved from simple systems to larger, complex systems of systems. When I retired, I was responsible for the airplane network group adapting commercial ethernet to aviation and cyber security. None of these existed when I graduated, and looking back, I probably would not have taken that path. Over time, I worked in different roles and found what interested me. Then I made moves to follow that interest.

The advice I gave these up-and-coming leaders and engineering minds was to follow something that interests them and keeps their options open. If you hire into a large company like Boeing, you'll have ample opportunity to move into different roles within the company, which is much easier than leaving and looking for a new job.

I also counseled them, as they thought about their interests, to look at the big picture of jobs. Some jobs work with detailed design, some work with larger systems, and some explore new and novel technologies. If you struggle with detailed design, you should probably focus on those higher-level interests instead.

Once you narrow down a high-level interest, look for companies with those types of jobs and research them. Adapt your resume to highlight your knowledge of the position before you submit it. As a recruiter, I thought if someone took the time to put a few keywords into their resume, it showed they had read the job description. Their resume got pulled for further review.

The last bit of advice I gave the students was not to expect to get a management job immediately. We were hiring engineers, not managers. Getting into management in a highly technical field often takes five to ten years, depending on the job.

Once new hires were in the group, they were off and running, and we'd incorporate them into the performance review process. I always asked them if they were happy or if they would like an opportunity somewhere else. With the more seasoned engineers, I would ask, "What do you want to do when you grow up, move into management or a technical fellowship?"

Most didn't really answer, but I would ask them to think about it. One individual caught me probably three years later as I was walking by his desk. He said, "John, the question you asked me a few years ago…I have an answer—I want to be a technical fellow." I was a little surprised, but the question had made him think, and we did move him into the technical fellowship. These are decisions you will make as you progress in your career.

FOLLOW YOUR GUT

The second bit of advice I gave was to follow your gut, or as one of my bosses frequently said, "What does your Spidey sense tell you?" The science behind researching "gut feelings" was pioneered by neuroendocrinologist (a doctor specializing in brain chemistry) Dr. Deepak Chopra. He described his thoughts in the YouTube video, "Trust Your Gut Feeling a Little More." It's an interesting video discussing biological responses within your body and how all your cells are connected and communicating with each other.

I have relied on my gut several times. Once, I had a job opportunity I was really interested in, but my immediate boss counseled me not to pursue it. My gut told me to do it—it was in an area that I found interesting, it expanded my responsibilities, and involved more customer contact. I took the job.

I had some frustrations in that position like with any new job, but I learned a lot and was exposed to a completely different area. About a year later, I had the opportunity to be promoted to leading more teams than I already was. The teams did what the teams I was leading did, and I was the only candidate with that experience. I got the job. Had I not moved or followed my gut, I would not have had that experience nor the background that went beyond the other candidates.

Another time was when we purchased a new home in Coeur d'Alene, which would involve moving from the Seattle area to Idaho. On the evening of the home inspection, I didn't sleep a bit. I was tossing and turning, and my gut was upset. I woke up and told Bonnie I couldn't do it. I called the realtor and told him we were backing out. Suddenly, I was relaxed and calm. I'm not sure if it was a good or bad decision, but I didn't follow through with it.

I believe your gut is your body's way of helping you along as you encounter significant decisions or situations.

STRUCTURED INTERVIEWS

When I started interviewing potential employees, it was an informal affair. I was given training, and we pretty much asked any questions we wanted. The key was knowing which questions were off limits and ensuring you asked all candidates the same questions. We would ask questions about their resume, maybe some technical questions, and some questions to gauge their interests. We would then take the candidates' interview results back to the office and decide whom to follow up with and give offers to. This was the manager's decision. I interviewed one candidate in a hotel lobby and a second at dinner.

Somewhere along the way, the lawyers got involved in ensuring corporations had a fair and consistent process. We were given pretty specific guidance on how to conduct interviews. The primary change was to move to a more behavioral set of questions instead of technical ones. Many companies did this, and at a certain level, it made sense. These questions gauged how potential candidates behaved in different situations—how they dealt with difficult people, what they found challenging, and how they addressed it. These questions also helped determine which candidates worked well in a team. Most jobs today require interaction with other departments or engineers.

Structured interviews are common now among large companies prior to a deeper technical evaluation. A diverse interview panel is set up to ask and evaluate the questions. The key to success in a structured interview is to prepare by thinking about how you'd answer these kinds of questions and how you interact with people and solve problems.

PEOPLE BUY AIRPLANES

Toward the end of my career, many of the people I'd been working with for many years were planning to retire. One of them, Dan, did some research and started having seminars on retirement that gathered very large crowds at lunchtime. I attended one, saw the numbers, and jokingly said, "Everyone back to work…nobody is retiring!" The lunch sessions were quite informative, and I even volunteered later to give a presentation on setting up an estate plan—medical, financial, and the traditional will.

In the presentations, Dan described what it took to retire, how much money you would probably need, and some commentary on life after Boeing. He also decided to sponsor other lunchtime forums and invited senior leadership to discuss their careers and take questions. Dan even had the fortitude to invite the president of the Boeing Commercial Airplane Company. Dan didn't know him, but he asked—what could he say—no? He said yes.

The president of Boeing showed up with a security detail and in a private car. He had started at Boeing as a machinist and worked his way up through sales, ultimately becoming the president. He was very interesting to listen to because of his sales background and experiences none of us had had. One thing he said really stuck with me, and I have repeated it many times: "Airlines don't buy airplanes; people at the airlines do." His message was that it's all about personal relationships. He even told a story about an airline CEO who was getting pressure from his board to drop some Boeing orders. Based on the CEO's relationship with Boeing's president, the CEO pushed back and kept the order—and never regretted it.

As I said earlier, as you travel through your career, you will meet all sorts of people. Some who work for you and some you work for. That can change quickly since you may end up working for people who once worked with you or for you. Remember the story of the manager who didn't see the potential in some of the up-and-coming engineers who later became his superiors. He hadn't treated them with respect when he was over them. He paid later when they were in control of his advancement. You'll interact with many every day, and your "gut" may tell you some are destined for greater glory than others. It doesn't matter, though. Just follow the rule:

> *Treat everyone with respect and dignity. As time goes on, people will remember and help you out more readily, knowing your character and how they were treated.*

Second, find people who can teach you from all perspectives. You may typically look for mentors who are senior, but looking to someone junior to you can be just as valuable. I had a senior manager who was working in cyber security. He reached out to a couple of newer engineers to ask them to mentor him in cyber and related technology. All were rewarded—the senior manager learned the technology, and the engineers established a bond and a positive relationship with him.

Find someone who can help you present to and interact with people. Find someone who can help you put a plan together on what your future desires are. Find someone who can act as a sounding board to help you understand issues and guide you to a better decision. These don't have to be formal or documented mentorships. It can be as simple as a regular meeting or phone call to talk to them. I even found not having a strict agenda is helpful at times to let the conversation drift somewhat to what is currently on your mind or theirs.

Last, never turn down help. When you're working, you'll get into a bind, get a little behind, or not understand something. People are watching, and when they offer help, always accept it. It's hard at times for some people to admit they need help, but by accepting it readily, you send a message to your leadership that you will engage and are open to different points of view. If you refuse the help, the opposite may happen. You may continue having issues, and your leadership will take note that you didn't accept help; then in a worst-case scenario, they will bring someone else in to complete the task. I have seen both—always accept help.

Also, just because you accepted help doesn't mean the person offering can really help or even wants to. I've seen some people offer help knowing it will be rejected and then use that rejection in the future as critical feedback. I've experienced it myself. Therefore, if I had a very challenging task and my leadership, recognizing my challenges, offered "help," I would accept. Once accepted, the "helpers" would ask what they could do. I would give them a task or something I had an issue with, and more than half the time, they disappeared, providing no help at all. Even without their help, I was able to say with a straight face that I had accepted offers of help.

The overall point here is people will ultimately help you progress in your career. Your boss and other bosses choose who gets promoted. If they don't know who you are or your capabilities, you start off at a disadvantage. Unfortunately, you need to do some level of politicking, and you need to present yourself, your skills, and your willingness to work with others to those who will directly advance your career.

SKILL, LUCK, AND BEING IN THE RIGHT PLACE AT THE RIGHT TIME

I was always asked, "How did you get your job?" I was the executive responsible for network, cabin, and cyber technologies and had what I thought was the best job in the company. As you progress into management, you start at a first line position, leading groups from fifteen to thirty people. While this position is not easy to get, there are many of them. The next position is senior manager. The selection process gets much more stringent here and the pool of candidates much more qualified. I ended up being in an executive position, one that required the company board to approve. These positions are coveted, and many vice presidents have candidates they put forward, making it much more challenging to land a job at this level. One negative mark from a senior executive could prevent you from making it to that level. These are groups from 100 to 500 people, so the pool of candidates for a single position is large.

At Boeing, the management was technical, and everyone knew it. Significant positions were filled from within by candidates with an understanding of the technology. I was always a candidate for executive positions, but I never got selected—until cyber security became a hot issue. While I didn't plan it, I did volunteer to put a plan together for cyber security on a commercial airplane ten years prior and moved into the role—nobody was really focused on it early on. A couple of things happened in the industry, so the board decided to create an executive position, and I was selected.

Was I the only candidate who could have done the job? Probably not, but I was the only person with the right background. I also had a positive relationship with the senior executives who were going to make the selection. I had always worked on my presentation skills, keeping my message concise, and I had a good track record in resolving issues and understanding the technology in the area. Finally, I had the good luck to be working on cyber security at the time.

Why did I get the job? I had the right skills, I was in the right place when the job was created, and I had lucked out in picking a job path that led me there. My message here is:

- Understand your job (skills).
- Put yourself in positions where you can demonstrate your abilities (in the right place).
- Be flexible and able to change quickly to adapt to emerging trends and hope for the best (luck).

The vice president of engineering when I hired into Boeing essentially told us this when describing how he got his job, and many others since have said the same.

SUMMARY

I contend that many people probably start their careers or families not knowing what they really want. You could decide you want children and then think maybe you should have waited. Others may not want children but find out too late that they probably should have had some. The same is true when you start a job. With today's fast-paced technological advances, what you know now will be much different tomorrow. Understand this and, instead of a laser focus, pick a path; then as you travel down it, you'll learn things that will help you home in on where you want to be. Some want to be managers right off the bat, but after seeing what the management job really entails, decide it isn't their cup of tea.

Follow your gut. I believe it's your body and subconscious helping you along. Some believe there is a spiritual aspect as well. I can't answer either way, but I can say when I followed my gut (or Spidey sense), it was always the best path.

Life has formal and informal aspects. Make sure you can identify the formal aspects and treat them as such. A job interview is a formal affair. Always be yourself, but treat it formally and don't make light during it. I lost a job I thought was mine mostly based on the interview. I was informal and even told some subtle jokes while being interviewed. After the interview, the feedback was "Don't do that."

Remember, people buy airplanes, not airlines. Knowing and having a positive relationship with those who are in a position to help is critical. This includes everyone from the CEO of the airline to the janitor who cleans your office. It's people who do the work and will help make you successful.

Finally, when climbing the ladder, know your job, put yourself in jobs and positions where you can highlight your skills to others, and be flexible to adapt to emerging trends.

EXERCISES

1. What kinds of new technologies and jobs do you think will be created in the next 5-10 years?

    _____

    _____

    _____

    _____

    _____

    _____

    _____

2. Have you been in a situation where your gut told you to do something, but you didn't? How did it end up?

    _____

    _____

    _____

    _____

    _____

    _____

    _____

3.   Would you know how to get in front of the right people who could help you in your career? Would this be a good topic for a mentor or your direct manager?

_____

_____

_____

_____

_____

_____

CHAPTER 15

PLANE TALK

"If black boxes survive air crashes, why don't they
make the whole plane out of that stuff?"

— George Carlin, Comedian

THE MYSTERY OF AVIATION

I was introduced to aviation early. My father told me a story about how
his father had said he'd buy him a ski pass, and my father wrote back,
asking if he could use the money instead to get flying lessons. My grandfather thought it was a great idea and decided to get his pilot's license. By
the time I was six or seven, I was in the co-pilot's seat of my grandfather's
Beech Bonanza "flying" and later, in my father's Grumman Cheetah. I
was hooked.

I started flying as soon as I legally could, learning in my father's airplane.
I remember the sheer terror of my first solo, moving into excitement, and
finding freedom toward the end. Unbeknownst to me, the ritual at the
time was to cut the back of your T-shirt off after your solo and document
the flight. I should have known something was up when my mother had

me put on a different shirt before that lesson and came along that afternoon.

Later, I would face some extremely rough conditions in the air where you could barely maintain airspeed in the twilight flying into Bozeman. It was a little nerve-racking, but once, upon clearing the Bozeman Pass, the air smoothed out and all the lights of the valley lit up the cockpit in a unique and calming way. I clicked my mike five times to trigger the airport runway lights and watched them turn on, one-by-one, in a steady stream until the entire runway was lit. This was another magical event I will always remember.

In college, when Boeing came to recruit, I thought it would be pretty cool to see how they made the big planes—in my mind a 727 or 737. My interview consisted of a recruiter asking me questions about my first solo and other flying experiences. I was offered the job and accepted, only to be truly amazed the first time I saw a 747—it was a massive plane beyond my comprehension at the time. Even the factory was huge. I got lost walking around the floor and decided to climb up some ladders. Going up two sets of stairs, I found myself under a 747 wing being built!

Boeing has a huge footprint in the Seattle area, and at times, the locals, press, and politicians don't truly understand what this company represents or what they build. I had an employee quit and go to work for Microsoft. He called me a couple of months later to ask for some advice. Apparently, some of the Microsoft employees were giving him a hard time for having worked at Boeing. I told him not to put up with that and asked him what he had done at Boeing. He said he was an equipment engineer working in cabin systems. I said, "No, that was your job; that's not what you did. You preformed electromagnetic scans on 777 and 747 airplanes by placing antennae in the cabin and measuring to see if any energy created interference with critical or essential systems. You went on flight tests to determine system operations that included decompression simulations and abnormal flight scenarios. You are one of a handful of people who understood what it really takes to get a system certified for flight and ensured reliability of the product for international customers." I added, "Ask what they do. They probably write a subroutine for a larger program that may never see the light of day."

He called me back the next day and thanked me. Apparently, they didn't really understand what engineers at Boeing actually do.

ACCIDENT INVESTIGATION

One unique thing about aviation is the singular focus on safety. I alluded to it earlier, and it cannot be overstated. My first few years at Boeing, I was privy to many different issues and incidents within the commercial aviation system. There were airplanes that didn't transfer fuel correctly, some that had to divert and make emergency landings, and the like. Most didn't involve any loss of an airplane or loss of life but our scrutiny of the issue and what caused it was extensive. We looked at how it happened and put in place changes to systems or pilot procedures to ensure it didn't happen again.

Looking at the accident rate for commercial aviation tells the entire story. Over the time aviation has existed, the accident rates have come down dramatically, making flying the safest way to travel. Many track this statistic from ICAO (International Civil Aviation Organization), FAA (Federal Aviation Administration), EASA (European Union Aviation Safety

Agency), and other governmental safety and regulatory agencies. When an issue did cause a loss of life or airplane, an entire team at Boeing would assemble all the relevant experts and provide support to the governmental agency leading the investigation.

Many significant improvements arose from these investigations. Controlled flight into terrain and midair collisions resulted in new systems on airplanes to alert pilots of their positions relative to terrain and other airplanes, and these incidences went almost to zero. The FAA has a "COSP" (Continued Operational Safety Program) that looks at these issues as they arise, then focuses on the most significant issues that have arisen and how to mitigate them going forward.

PLANE TALK ABOUT LEADERSHIP

Probably one of the most interesting classes I took at Boeing was titled, "Plane Talk About Leadership." We all make decisions daily. Some are insignificant like what to have for breakfast, while others can be very significant. And many of our decisions do not have immediate results, so knowing whether it was the right decision or how it might affect future decisions can be elusive. In the context of the timeframe of an accident, the result of decisions was easy to identify. The class focused on decisions (or lack of thereof) and how they were connected to aircraft accidents.

We looked at probably ten different accidents. Behind each was a lesson we could use to prevent future accidents or mitigate their results. Over time, we have seen milestone accidents that changed aviation for the better. I have listed a few below, along with the high-level lesson or change that made aviation safer.

Not Making a Decision—Crew Resource Management

In 1978, the crew of an airline approaching Portland heard a loud thump from the landing gear. The indicator light was not illuminated, indicating the gear was not down and locked. The crew contacted the tower and did a fly by to see if the tower could see the position of the landing gear. The airplane went into a holding pattern to troubleshoot the problem. While troubleshooting, the airplane ran out of fuel and crashed in suburban Portland, killing ten of the 189 people aboard. This incident was the start of Crew Resource Management Training. Later, Captain Al Haynes, who landed a DC-10 in Sioux City, Iowa, after a critical loss of hydraulics, credited this training for being able to bring that airplane down. Although 112 of the 296 passengers and crew died in the crash, it is considered a prime example of crew resource management since it was the kind of situation where all onboard would likely have been lost in the past.

Conversion Factors

An airline was in the process of converting to metric measurements. The fuel gauge didn't provide the correct indication in metric, so the fuel was measured using a dripstick. (A dripstick is a hollow tube inserted into a commercial aircraft fuel tank to measure fuel levels.). When calculating the fuel volume, they mistakenly used pounds instead of kilograms. One-kilogram weighs two-point-two pounds so they had about half the fuel they thought they had. This airplane ran out of fuel while flying over Canada. The captain knew of an abandoned airstrip and was able to successfully land the airplane without power.

Not Listening to All Information Presented

A Middle Eastern airline had a smoke detector go off in the cargo compartment and then cleared. Feedback from the rear of the airplane indicated a lot of smoke, but the captain did not declare an emergency. With the smoke in the rear of the airplane, it was not apparent in the flight deck. The pilot did turn back, but when asked if they needed an emergency evacuation, did not respond. The airplane landed with emergency equipment ready at the airport, but they did not execute an emergency stop, and when they arrived at the end of the two-mile runway, they did not shut down the engines. With the engines running, the ground crew could not approach the airplane. All onboard perished from the incident.

No Smoking in the Lavatories

In 1983, an airplane had thick black smoke coming out of its lavatory. Barely seeing the instruments, the pilots were able to land the airplane, but when the airplane doors were opened, it released a flash fire. Based on this, the FAA mandated smoke detectors in lavatories, fire blocking in the cabin, and floor lighting to the exits.

Midair Collisions

In 1956, two aircraft collided over the Grand Canyon. All 128 passengers were killed, and it spurred a $250,000,000 upgrade to the air traffic control system. Later in 1986, a small airplane wandered into the Los Angeles control area colliding with a DC-9. This caused the FAA to mandate transponders on small aircraft reporting position and altitude. After this, the FAA mandated new collision avoidance systems with improvements. These types of midair collisions have not occurred in the United States since.

Many more incidents have occurred, each investigated in great detail by regulatory agencies. The reports are available for public review. All these accidents resulted in changes to the airplanes and/or aviation system to preclude such incidents in the future. This is why flying is by far the safest way to travel.

BOEING FACILITIES

I was fortunate to participate in the design and build of several Boeing airplanes over my thirty-five years there. These included the end of the 747-400, delivery of the first 777 and 747-8 airplanes, and participating in the 787 program. Building airplanes is a very capital-intensive and risky business. Reportedly, the company bet its future on the 707 and original 747 programs and put billions into development of the more recent airplanes. Not only do you have to fund development and build of the airplane, but you also need to build the facilities to do it. The Everett Factory is the largest building in the world when measured by volume. It is 98.3 acres and around ten stories tall. It has six doors measuring eighty-two-feet tall with the original doors measuring 300 feet wide. The two newest doors are 350 feet wide. An American football field, by comparison, is 160 by 360 feet. Inside the building, you can fit Disneyland and all its parking lots. Even the murals on the doors are the largest digital graphics on the planet.

The factory was built in the late 1960s in unison with the design of the original 747 airplanes. The people working there were termed the "Incredibles" for building the airplane in the facility while it was under construction. Over time, the building expanded, with the latest expansion taking place in the 1990s for the 777 airplane.

There are many interesting and unique things about the factory. First, there is no heating or cooling system. Being in the Pacific Northwest, the temperature is moderate, and adjusting for heating or cooling is accomplished by opening the doors. Another interesting fact is when the original factory was built, it developed its own weather system with clouds and, at times, rain. This was solved by putting an air distribution system into the factory to circulate the air from the ceiling to floor. With a building this size, the mechanical systems are large as well and are in a series of tunnels underneath the factory floor. These tunnels also serve as passageways for employees going between areas in the factory and outside buildings. There is a "road" in the middle of the factory that goes from one end to the other called main street. It is seven-tenths of a mile with similar roads perpendicular to it at around three-tenths of a mile. Everything in this building is large, and timing meetings in the building or in the onsite engineering buildings needs to be considered. While I was working in the factory, I had a bike and used it to get from place to place in the building. (I had some enthusiastic employees who decided to decorate it with a pink basket and pink streamers. When I rode it in the factory, it was noticed a couple of times by my superiors.)

Moving parts in this building are also big. One crane system can move a fuselage section or wing from one area to another. I had a desk in the middle of the factory on the top floor of the engineering towers next to a window that looked down onto the factory floor. Probably one of the coolest things I saw was when a crane came by the window moving an airplane fuselage. I would get up and alert the group that the crane was just outside—many thought I was crazy, but that kind of stuff never got old.

With the windows looking into the factory, I would take dry erase markers and sketch out different ideas on the windows. One day, it dawned on me that the windows on the factory side were a little dirty. To be funny, I called a ticket into facilities to have my windows cleaned. They weren't sure how to handle it, and they investigated how to do it. We didn't really have window cleaners on ropes coming by the engineering towers on a schedule to clean our windows. When I moved out of the factory a year later, the windows were still dirty.

Working in this factory was really a special thing that, over time, we all took for granted. We would get all sorts of visitors and dignitaries, and the one thing they all wanted was a VIP tour of the factory. Even today, you can take the Boeing tour, but you will only get to see the factory from a couple of balconies overlooking the production line. There is nothing like walking under a wing or standing next to landing gear being staged for installation. I would encourage my group to walk through the factory and really get a feel for what we were building and our part in it. Few people have had this experience, and I feel fortunate to have been one of them.

DESIGNING AIRPLANES

Large commercial jet airliner design is a very complex and integrated process. The entire cycle can last four to five years, followed by a lifetime of improvements and addressing in-service issues to make the airplane more reliable. With an airplane being a very expensive item (a new 777-9 airplane can cost $400 to $500 million depending on options and specific configurations), purchasing one is a major decision for an airline. The entire process starts with a market analysis of what may be needed. You have to answer the question: Do you build a large airplane (747 or A380) to fly to hubs, or a smaller airplane (787 or A350) to do more of a direct flight?

In his book 747, Joe Sutter, the chief engineer for the program, discusses how Pan Am came to Boeing asking for a larger airplane—almost double the size of the then current 707 or DC-8 airplanes (around 140 passengers). Pam Am concluded they needed a 350-passenger airplane. Naturally, everyone started thinking about a double-decker, including the Boeing team who had a C-5 military transport proposal that had a double deck. (They lost the contract to the competition.) In evaluating the proposals for different configurations, Boeing decided to look at a single deck with a configuration with ten passengers across in economy. This was not popular, and Boeing executives were worried that Pan Am might not like it. Boeing scheduled a meeting with Pan Am, to which Boeing staff took a twenty-foot clothesline. Upon arriving at the meeting room at Pan Am, they found the conference room was twenty feet wide. During the meeting, they pulled out the rope and gave a visual description of what they were proposing. This became the world's first widebody, the iconic 747—Queen of the Skies.

A big part of design is getting the airlines involved and in concurrence with the airplane you are proposing. Once these larger questions are answered, the process starts to go into a lower level of detail, in a tiered fashion. We call this the engineering "V" where high-level requirements are translated into lower-level requirements, ultimately getting to a level of detail where you can start designing and building parts. This is the bottom of the V. On the way back up, you test the lower-level designs, the systems elements, and then test the integrated systems that represent the airplane. The ultimate test is when the airplane is completed and goes through a very thorough test program to verify the structural elements, systems performance, and flight characteristics, and meets the airline's operational requirements. Along the way, we find problems and we ask ourselves, "Is it an error in the design or build? Or is it an error in the requirements?" Once identified, we make a change to correct the problem. In the end, all the requirements from the high level to low level have been validated. Not many industries are this thorough.

ENGINEERING FLIGHT TEST

One of the best parts of designing an airplane is getting to participate in flight testing and system checkout on the flight line. The flight line is a very active space with airplanes in different states of build. On the 747 program, the practice was to start the engines in the flight line stalls and power out using thrust. The idea was to give it some high thrust to get the airplane moving until it is out of the stall and on the taxiway. While working on an airplane, a customer was at the controls of the airplane and didn't follow this protocol. With a 747 engine developing upwards of 56,000 pounds of thrust, you need to be careful about what is behind the airplane, something probably not obvious while in the flight deck. As the airplane moved out of the stall and started to turn, the pilot did not reduce thrust and the engine blast hit a pickup, tore off a canopy on the back bed, and slammed it into the doghouse for the stall. I kind of chuckled at it, but the guy next to me looked at me and said, "That's not funny; that's my truck." Airplanes are now towed to the runway due to these kinds of random incidents.

In flight tests, we test the airplane to its limit and a little beyond. This includes checking the noise in the cabin, flutter tests to check the structure, aerodynamic tests to check fuel economy, rejected takeoffs, and others. This is a very disciplined and formal process where the engineering teams define the test, a ground operations team organizes the test, and a flight test team conducts the test.

There are all sorts of different tests that are run both on the ground in a lab and during flight. Some are pretty mundane while others are more unique. A good example is the diaper test in the lavatories. Mothers on flights may decide to flush a full diaper, so the system needed to take this into account. While testing, some young engineers took dog food, put it in the diaper, and placed it into the toilet. They flushed it and it went down easily. It worked like a charm until one of the managers noticed.

Dan asked, "Do any of you have kids? That is not how you dispose of a full diaper." He then took the diaper, put dog food in it, and wrapped it up in a tight ball. He then put it into the toilet and pressed the flush button. The system made all sorts of noises, shook, and vibrated until there was almost a shotgun blast when the suction of the toilet finally pulled the wrapped-up ball into the tank. He looked at the engineers and said, "Looks like it passes that test."

Another test done during flight is a noise test to measure the ambient noise in the cabin during the different phases of flight—something the airline was very interested in. When tests are conducted during flight, usually several are done at the same time to optimize the flight. I've been on several flights where before the flight starts, box lunches are provided. These box lunches come with different sandwiches or salads so you want to get yours early or you may get one you don't really like. On a particular day, a noise test was scheduled while we were testing the inflight entertainment system. I was one of the first onto the airplane—I grabbed my lunch of choice and hid it from everyone else. I then hid it in an oven in the galley (they were never used during most tests). Unfortunately, on a noise test, the ovens are turned on and my box lunch was heated up to the point where much of it was not edible. I was also chastised by the flight test crew for putting it in the ovens to begin with. (Although on an earlier flight, these same folks had given me the idea.)

THE CHICKEN CANNON

One of the more interesting tests verifies different parts of the airplane can withstand a bird strike. Bird strikes do happen, with one of the more famous being a US Airways Airbus A320 that lost thrust in both engines in New York over the Hudson River. The airplane had collided with a flock of Canada geese and Captain Chesley "Sully" Sullenberger ditched the airplane in the Hudson, saving all 155 people onboard.

During an inflight entertainment industry meeting at Disney studios, I gave a presentation and made a comment at the end about the requirement of shooting a chicken cannon at the internet radome on the crown of the airplane. I sat down. When the next speaker began his presentation, one of the media folks interrupted to ask, "You don't really shoot chickens at airplanes do you?" I said, "Yes, we do." I had a video of the actual test itself to show them later that day. If you search the internet, you'll see this question asked and answered, even with a reference to *Myth Busters*. I can attest that we do, indeed, shoot dead chickens at airplanes. (Well, we now use a facsimile of one due to feedback from animal lovers.)

Chickens are shot at engines at full thrust while testing at the engine manufacturer. The military and commercial airplane manufacturers shoot them at the cockpit windows to ensure they will not penetrate the cockpit, and my group required the test for radomes on the crown of the airplane. The chickens are shot from a pneumatic gun and can develop speeds of 250 to 350 feet per second. I have read that the military shoot them faster.

My part in all this was the passenger internet system on the airplane. The Ku/Ka satellite antennas on commercial airplanes are easy to spot at airports. Look at almost any airplane and you'll probably see one. A radome is the size of a small, inverted canoe. The dome protects the antenna mechanism on the crown of the airplane. The requirement is the structural elements of the radome must withstand a bird strike. In the test, the radome cannot come loose or break apart in a way that could damage the tail. Early on, designing a radome that could withstand the test was a challenge, but now it is commonplace for these systems. As I write, this technology is undergoing significant change with a move from geo-stationary satellites 22,500 miles above the surface to low earth orbit ones at 1,200 miles. This allows smaller antenna and terminals to interface with them.

SUMMARY

I was hooked on aviation from the moment I sat in my grandfather's airplane. My brother and I purchased a large boat a while back, but it wasn't the same. While a boat brings a level of freedom, it doesn't compare to an airplane. In an airplane, you get a view of the terrain from the sky, can see miles ahead, and get to your destination much faster.

Aviation is a somewhat small community with many of the same people in their same roles at a company or moving to other companies to take similar ones. I spent thirty-five years at the Boeing Company, and after retirement, I am still working in aviation part time. Being a part of the design, build, and testing of a large commercial airplane is not something many can claim. I have come to love these airplanes, the discipline that goes into designing and building them, and being an integral part of some of the systems installed on them. Coming from Montana and walking into the largest building in the world was overwhelming, and when we hosted people, it was a highlight of their visit, something they could not do anywhere else in the world. Just the capital investment required and the risk that companies take across aviation is impressive and something I've been proud to have been a part of. Every day leaving work when I was stationed in the factory, I would walk out on the floor where 747s, 777s, 767s, and 787s were being built. It never got old for me.

Technology is ever-moving, and this new technology finds its way into aviation designs and connectivity options. While some companies develop technology for the massive consumer market, what we put in the airplane has to be brought up to aviation standards, followed by a disciplined incorporation into the airplane.

As with everything, nothing is perfect, and aviation is no different. Where aviation is different, though, is in the time and effort that goes into in-service issues and accident investigation. Everyone involved, from regulators, airframe manufacturers, and suppliers, has a unique focus on finding root causes and implementing fixes to ensure issues don't arise again. Part of this is a rigorous test regime which, in my area, included a chicken cannon.

Just think about it on your next flight across the United States. It would take six months in a covered wagon. By stagecoach it was twenty-five days. It wasn't until the transcontinental railroad was completed that it moved to around four or five days. A non-stop flight from New York City to Los Angeles today is around six hours, and you can fly to the other side of the world in about eighteen hours. One can only wonder how we'll transit the world in 100 years. And it all started just a little over a century ago with the advent of aviation and technology.

EXERCISES

1. What kind of "chicken cannon" test do you use when working on projects? Do you look for ways to test your activities to ensure they are robust?

    _____

    _____

    _____

    _____

2. What do you do when you make an error or mistake? Do you analyze what happened and try to ensure it doesn't happen again?

    _____

    _____

    _____

    _____

A FINAL NOTE

You've come to the end of this book. I hope you have taken notes and thought about what actions you can take to help you going forward. While the exercises at the end of each chapter focused on the lessons in that chapter, I hope they helped you to reflect on the situations and how they might be similar to situations you've been in.

I challenge you to take note of some of these lessons and incorporate them into your daily life. From Dr. Phil to some of the things I stumbled on over time, you can start doing some things today that will make a difference. Start off easy. Make eye contact with the server, ask people to do things instead of telling them to, be respectful, and have empathy. These are simple things, but things we sometimes don't realize the importance of until the moment has passed. When I changed how I interacted with people and groups, I noticed the difference immediately—and the people I interacted with changed how they perceived me, in a good way.

I have left space for you to list some actions you are going to take going forward.

- _____

- _____

- _____

- _____
- _____
- _____
- _____
- _____
- _____
- _____
- _____
- _____
- _____
- _____

I've included many lessons in this book, with some common themes. These are all things I learned the hard way, and many I wish I would have understood earlier.

- Everyone is unique and should be treated with respect, even if they don't respond in kind. Roles will generally reverse over time, and as the saying goes, "Don't burn your bridges behind you."

- People are always watching you. People will judge you, and their initial perception will form very fast.

- Always do the right thing, even if it's risky. One of my bosses said frequently, "You can't manage a secret." The same is true for a lie. When you tell the truth, it's much easier to remember.

- Technology continues to change our world, our culture, and how we interact. Be flexible.

- Planning and getting the foundation correct upfront will make the rest of your life much easier, even if it takes more effort than originally planned.

- Recognize everyone and realize all have an important place in our lives. Whether it's the parking lot attendant, janitor, or waiter at a restaurant, they all have more power over our lives than we may realize.

- Always accept help and offer it when warranted. That is how you grow and help others grow.

- Be confident in your abilities.

In this book, we discussed all these lessons, starting with interactions with people, some of whom may not like us. I discussed how as a leader we are being watched, and our actions will speak larger than our words. We always must do the right thing. The key to succeeding is building a plan with a solid foundation. We need to recognize others and offer and receive help whenever needed.

Finally, be confident in yourself. Nobody is perfect, but if you can recognize this and move beyond your faults, you will succeed.

COOL YOUTUBE VIDEOS

The stories in my book are from my firsthand experience, but I used You-Tube and other social media sites for background or parallel stories to reenforce the messages. Social media is a powerful medium that can provide a wealth of knowledge if used with caution. Every effort was made to validate all claims in the book and provide a general reference when using such claims. Below are some videos and references I used both at work and at home to convey these messages.

- Louis CK on "Everything Is Amazing" and "Nobody Is Happy"
- Simon Sinek on "Millennials in the Workplace"
- Stuxnet—"Anatomy of a Computer Virus"
- "Amazing Mind Reader Reveals His 'Gift'"
- Inno-Versity Presents "Greatness" by David Marquet (based on his book, *Turn This Ship Around*)
- Regent Law Professor James Duane on "Don't Talk to the Police"
- Dr. Deepak Chopra on "Trust Your Gut Feeling a Little More"

Reference:

747 Creating the World's First Jumbo Jet and Other Adventures from a Life in Aviation by Joe Sutter

ABOUT THE AUTHOR

John Craig is a widely-recognized aviation expert and executive engineering leader with more than thirty-five years of aerospace experience. John has held a series of key positions, including Chief Engineer at Boeing, where he was responsible for cabin systems, onboard networks, and cyber security for all commercial airplanes. In this role, he was the Chief Information Security Officer for Commercial Airplanes and developed vast experience in aircraft systems. John is a licensed Professional Engineer for the State of Washington, prior Federal Aviation Administration Designated Engineering Representative, and while at Boeing, was a member of the RTCA Policy Board and Program Management Committee. Creating the cyber security function for commercial airplanes, he worked to establish the Aviation Information Sharing and Analysis Center and was its first Board Chairman until his departure from Boeing.

Growing up in Montana provided John with unique experiences and a level of freedom to learn how to think outside the box and solve problems with limited resources. He learned to fly at an early age following in the footsteps of his father and grandfather as private pilots. He graduated from Montana State University with a Bachelor of Science in Electrical Engineering and started work right out of college at the Boeing Company, working from the start on commercial airplanes.

John has attended and been a keynote speaker at many industry conferences. He has a wealth of knowledge and experience not only in aviation, but in the managerial and personality challenges of both homelife and the workplace.

BOOK JOHN CRAIG TO SPEAK

When it comes to choosing a professional speaker for your next event, you will find John Craig a powerful speaker with stories of aviation and leadership told from firsthand experience. His leadership skills and industry knowledge will provide your audience or colleagues a unique opportunity to get a glimpse inside the aviation industry and learn leadership lessons that go well beyond aviation. And some stories will just make you smile.

John has presented to audiences from 10 to 1,000 and been asked many times to speak at industry events. If you are looking for a memorable speaker, book John Craig today.

john@johncraigconsulting.com
JohnCraigConsulting.com
JohnCraigLessons.com
LifeLessonsLearnedTheHardWay.com